I CAN HEAL

STORIES OF REAL DOCTORS. REAL SACRIFICES. REAL IMPACT

VOLUME I

THE DOCTORPRENEUR ACADEMY
Empowering Doctors to Serve Humanity Better

Chennai • Bangalore

CLEVER FOX PUBLISHING
Chennai, India

Published by CLEVER FOX PUBLISHING 2025
Copyright © The Doctorpreneur Academy 2025

All Rights Reserved.
ISBN: 978-93-67074-23-7

This book has been published with all reasonable efforts taken to make the material error-free after the consent of the author. No part of this book shall be used, reproduced in any manner whatsoever without written permission from the author, except in the case of brief quotations embodied in critical articles and reviews.

The Author of this book is solely responsible and liable for its content including but not limited to the views, representations, descriptions, statements, information, opinions and references ["Content"]. The Content of this book shall not constitute or be construed or deemed to reflect the opinion or expression of the Publisher or Editor. Neither the Publisher nor Editor endorse or approve the Content of this book or guarantee the reliability, accuracy or completeness of the Content published herein and do not make any representations or warranties of any kind, express or implied, including but not limited to the implied warranties of merchantability, fitness for a particular purpose. The Publisher and Editor shall not be liable whatsoever for any errors, omissions, whether such errors or omissions result from negligence, accident, or any other cause or claims for loss or damages of any kind, including without limitation, indirect or consequential loss or damage arising out of use, inability to use, or about the reliability, accuracy or sufficiency of the information contained in this book.

CONTENTS

Foreword .... *vii*
Acknowledgement .... *ix*
List of Contributing Authors .... *xi*
Introduction .... *xix*

1. How I Started and established my Homeopathic Practice in Kanpur 1
   Dr. Alkab Hasan Nazar,
2. The Secret to Running a Successful Dental Practice! 6
   Dr. Amit Patil
3. Running a hospital is more than just providing medical care 12
   Dr Arjun Hosalli
4. How Acupressure Changed Lives – My Journey of Healing from the Heart 17
   Ashvini Atre Kulkarni
5. Initial Struggles to Success: Journey of all Dentists 24
   Dr. Atindra Das
6. The Heartbeat of Change: My Journey from Farmland to Cardiology 29
   Dr Birendra Kumar
7. Struggles, Strength & Success – My Life-Changing Story 33
   Dr Chitra Patil
8. My Rapid Career Rise in Ophthalmology – A Journey of Vision and Growth 37
   Dr Devanshi Shah

Contents

9. How to Start and Grow a Hospital Successfully. 42
   Dr. Dilip Gupta
10. From Small-Town Surgeon to Healthcare Leader! 48
    Dr. Dinesh Sharma
11. Doctors, read This Real Story Before You Start Your Own Hospital! 52
    Dr. Gangambika
12. A doctor's Journey from 0 to 1,00,000 subscribers on YouTube 56
    Dr. G Buvaneswari,
13. The Green Doctor: Healing with Nature, Not Just Medicine 62
    Dr. Jaya Chandra Mohan
14. A Gynaecologist Teaching Moms Online! 67
    Dr. Jyoti MD DGO
15. Real Heroes: How We Brought Modern Healthcare to a Village—Our Journey of Heart, Grit & Vision 72
    Dr Kailas Sanamadikar
    Dr Vaishali Sanamadikar
16. A Journey of Resilience, Reinvention, and Wellness: My Story ... 77
    Dr Kavita Jain
17. Dr. Kiran Ambekar's Ayurvedic Wisdom – Helping Patients Naturally 83
    Dr. Kiran Ambekar
18. From Small Town Doctor to YouTube Star: My Journey Dr Kishan Bhagwat 87
    Dr. Kishan R. Bhagwat
19. Incredible Journey of FRCS to Founder: My Journey Back Home 91
    Dr. Manjunath

20. On a Mission for a Deafness Free India by 2047 95
    Dr. Manoj Kumar Gupta.
21. Doctor to Entrepreneur: How I Did It! 101
    Dr. Manoj Kumar
22. A Dream Rooted in My Hometown to Serve the Motherland 106
    Dr. Muralidhara, MBBS, MS, DNB
23. From the First Urologist in Kolhapur to a Healthcare Visionary 110
    Dr. Narendra Basarge
24. Real Solutions for Fixing Hospitals & Training Doctors 116
    Dr. Neeraj Bedi
25. How I transformed my clinic into a patient magnet! 120
    Dr. Neeraj Saraswat
26. Why Every Doctor Must Do Branding 124
    Dr Neha Singhania
27. Struggles to Success in Healthcare-My story of a healer 130
    Dr Nirmala Agarwal
28. How I established a pediatric super-speciality hospital in less than 6 months with few loan liabilities 134
    Dr. Nitin Agrawal
29. How Digital Tools Helped Me Grow My Eye Clinic – My Journey, Dr. Pankaj 139
    Dr. Pankaj Goswami
30. How I Made a Difference as a Dentist in Remote India – Dr. Pankaj Kohli's Story 144
    Dr.Pankaj Kohli BDS, FETP
31. From Average Student to Community Leader in the field of Ayurveda– My Doctorpreneur Journey 148
    By Vaidya Sanjay Maheshwari

32. Cancer Surgeon balancing Work, Family, and Faith 154
    Dr. Satish Kamat
33. Start Early. Heal Deep. Think Different. The Truth About
    Psychiatry: What They Don't Tell You 159
    Dr. Shubham Sabarwal
34. Doctor. Leader. Dreamer. The Story of a Woman Who
    Built a Legacy — In My Own Words 167
    Dr. Shubhangi Mundhada
35. How Social Media Transformed My Dermatology
    Practice – My Story as Dr. Sivaranjani 172
    Dr. Sivaranjani
36. From Government Duty to Private Practice: My Journey of
    Service, Growth & Legacy 176
    Dr. S. R. Sharma
37. Redefining Women's Healthcare Through Innovation,
    Resilience & Leadership 181
    Dr. Sumana Talakokkula
38. The Power of Dedication & Family Support in My Journey
    as a Surgeon, Mentor, and Human 186
    Dr. Suneet Sud
39. Pioneering Healthcare: My Journey from Clinician to
    Innovator Entrepreneur 190
    Dr. T J Pradeep Kumar
40. From Homemaker to Healthcare CEO: My Journey
    Behind Vardhan Fertility's Growth 195
    Vaibhavi, CEO

About The Doctorpreneur Academy 202
Founders of The Doctorpreneur Academy 205

FOREWORD

*I*n every hospital corridor, behind every consultation room, and beyond every prescription pad, lies a deeper truth: doctors are not just healers of individuals—they are potential architects of a healthier world.

We founded *The Doctorpreneur Academy* with a dream—to empower doctors to reclaim their voice, amplify their impact, and bring innovation into a system that often resists change. Over the past few years, we've had the privilege of mentoring thousands of doctors across all streams and specialisations, who didn't just want to practice medicine—they wanted to *transform* it.

This book, *I Can Heal*, is a tribute to them.

It is a collection of stories from real doctors—our peers, our students, our fellow dreamers—who have chosen courage over comfort. From remote towns to bustling metros, these doctors dared to imagine a new way to serve. They built hospitals and clinics when there were none. They pioneered specialty practices in underserved regions. They turned Instagram handles into health hubs and LinkedIn profiles into platforms for awareness and education.

Every page of this book is a reminder that **medicine is evolving**, and so are its messengers. These stories are not textbook case studies. These are lived experiences—rich with emotion, grit, and the kind of clarity that only comes from walking a difficult path. Their journeys show us that you don't need to be born with resources or a business degree to make an impact. What you do need is vision, integrity, and the belief that **healing is not a job—it's a mission.**

We hope that this book will serve as more than just inspiration. We hope it becomes a spark for your own transformation. Whether you're a fresh graduate wondering what lies beyond the clinic or a seasoned practitioner seeking meaning beyond the routine, this is your invitation to think bigger.

To serve is human.

To heal is divine.

To do both—that is the heart of the Doctorpreneur.

We dedicate *I Can Heal* to every doctor who has dared to dream differently—and to you, the leader, who may just be next.

With respect and belief,

Dr. Pranav Sharma
MBBS, MS, MCh (CTVS, AIIMS, Delhi)

&

Mr. Amit Singh Moga
B.Tech (IIT Roorkee), MBA (IIM Ahmedabad),
Ph.D (Healthcare, France)
Co-Founders, The Doctorpreneur Academy
(https://www.thedoctorpreneuracademy.com)

ACKNOWLEDGEMENT

*T*his book is not just a compilation of stories—it is a manifestation of faith, support, and a collective belief.

We bow in gratitude to the **Almighty**, whose invisible hand has guided us at every turn, opening doors, sending the right people, and blessing us with strength when we needed it most.

To all our gurus and teachers, who have been our guiding light and unwavering source of inspiration. Without their vision, we would not have been able to travel so far.

We thank **our parents**, whose unwavering confidence in us became the foundation on which we dared to dream. A special mention to **our mothers**, whose gentle hope lit our path even in the darkest moments—their belief has been our anchor. Though they are not physically present, they are still blessing us along the path shown by the Almighty.

To our **spouses**, thank you for your unspoken understanding, your patience, and for standing by us through the chaos of creation. And to our **children**, your laughter, mischief, and innocence kept the mood light and our hearts grounded throughout this journey.

We also express our heartfelt gratitude to our **extended families and friends**, whose quiet encouragement and consistent presence have been a source of strength behind the scenes. Your love and belief in our vision gave us the courage to keep moving forward.

Acknowledgement

A heartfelt thanks to the **40 doctors who shared their stories**—your courage, vulnerability, and victories form the soul of this book. You are living proof that healing goes far beyond medicine.

To **each and every member of the Doctorpreneur Academy**, thank you for being a constant source of **inspiration, energy, and encouragement**. Your passion to serve, your willingness to grow, and your trust in this mission make this community truly special and unstoppable.

A special note of appreciation to the **entire team at The Doctorpreneur Academy**. You rallied together, worked tirelessly, and brought this project to life in record time. Your dedication is what made *I Can Heal* more than just a book—it's now a movement.

To the entire fraternity of DOCTORS, you are the true change-makers—the heartbeat of a healthier tomorrow. Your dedication, compassion, and relentless pursuit of healing are shaping the future of the Indian Healthcare Ecosystem.

As you read these words, may they stir something deep within—a spark of inspiration, a tear of purpose, and an unstoppable drive to be part of something greater. "I CAN HEAL" is more than just a book series. It is a movement. A revolution. A call to awaken the limitless healer within each of us.

Together, we will empower, uplift, and transform lives.

One patient, one doctor, one breakthrough at a time.

With heartfelt gratitude and unwavering commitment,

Dr. Pranav Sharma

Mr. Amit Singh Moga
Co-Founders, The Doctorpreneur Academy

LIST OF CONTRIBUTING AUTHORS

1. Dr. Alkab Hasan Nazar

Homeopathy practitioner
Kanpur
nazarhomoeoclinic@gmail.com

2. Dr. Amit Patil

BDS, MDS in Maxillo-Facial Prosthodontics,
Implant Surgery & Cosmetic Dentistry, Goa
dr.amitpatil@gmail.com

3. Dr Arjun Hosalli

MBBS, MD (Internal Medicine), FCCM
Consultant Physician and Intensivist
Gangavathi, Karnataka
arjun.hosalli@gmail.com

4. Ashvini Atre Kulkarni

Acupressure Expert and Licensed Acupuncturist by certification
Pune
ashvini.s.atre2@gmail.com

5. Dr. Atindra Das

Dental Surgeon & tobacco cessation expert
Jagiroad, Assam
das.atindra@gmail.com

6. Dr Birendra Kumar

MBBS, MD, DM Cardiologist
Bhagalpur, Bihar
kbirendra97@gmail.com

7. Dr Chitra Patil

BAMS, Ayurveda and Quantum Healing Expert
Bengaluru, Karnataka
drchitra.rc@gmail.com

8. Dr Devanshi Shah

MS, Gold Medalist, DNB FNERF (Oculoplasty) FRCS UK.
Ophthalmologist
Mumbai
Devanshi.shah.333@gmail.com

9. Dr. Dilip Gupta

MBBS, MS Orthopedics
Basti, UP
drdilipbasti@gmail.com

10. Dr. Dinesh Sharma

MBBS MS ORTHO
Orthopedic Surgeon
Haryana
sharama_pooja@rediffmail.com

11. Dr. Gangambika

Gynecologist
Talikoti Karnataka
patilganga45@gmail.com

12. Dr. G Buvaneswari.

MBBS, DGO, DNB - Obstetrics & Gynecology
Infertility Specialist, Laparoscopic Surgeon (Obs & Gyn)
Chennai, Tamil Nadu gbuvaneswari@gbrclinic.com

13. Dr. Jaya Chandra Mohan

MBBS MD (ANESTHESIA), Natural healer
Narayanpet, Telangana
drkjcm@yahoo.com

14. Dr. Jyoti

MD DGO, Obstetrician and Gynecologist
Thrissur, Kerala
drjyotisenoj@gmail.com

15. Dr Kailas Sanamadikar (MBBS D.Ortho) & Dr Vaishali Sanamadikar (BAMS MD, Ayurveda)

Village Jath, District Sangli
Maharashtra
kailassanamadikar@gmail.com

16. Dr Kavita Jain

MBBS, DGO
Obstetrician and Gynecologist
New Delhi
drkavitajain09@gmail.com

17. Dr. Kiran Ambekar

BAMS, Consulting Ayurvedic physician, Mumbai
kiran.ambekar@gmail.com

18. Dr. Kishan R. Bhagwat

MBBS, MS (Ortho – PGI Chandigarh),
DNB (Ortho), MCh (Ortho), DipSICOT (Belgium)
CEO & Senior Consultant Orthopedic and Joint Replacement Surgeon,
Bhagwat Hospital, Sagar
kishan_bhagwat@yahoo.co.in

19. Dr. Manjunath

MS, FRCS Orthopedics
Tumkur, Karnataka
drgmanju@gmail.com

20. Dr. Manoj Kumar Gupta.

MBBS, MS(ENT)
ENT Surgeon, Educator, Author, and Mission-builder.
Varanasi, Uttar Pradesh
manoj2061@gmail.com

21. Dr. Manoj Kumar Sunar

MBBS, MS Gen. Surgery
Hissar, Haryana
m.manojsoni99@gmail.com

22. Dr. Muralidhara

MBBS, MS, DNB
Orthopedic surgeon
Tumkur, Karnataka
drmuralidhara@gmail.com

23. Dr. Narendra Basarge

Urologist,
MBBS & MS (General Surgery) M Ch (Urology),
Kolhapur, Maharashtra
narendra.basarge@gmail.com

24. Dr. Neeraj Bedi, MD PSM

Hospital Administrator
nbedi1202@gmail.com

25. Dr Neeraj Saraswat

Dentist and Implantologist
Jaipur
drsaraswat@gmail.com

26. Dr Neha Singhania

MS, DNB, MRCOG
Gynecologist, Mumbai
dr.nehasinghania@gmail.com

27. Dr Nirmala Agarwal

MBBS MD
Infertility and Gynecology Specialist
New Delhi
n.menoky@gmail.com

28. Dr. Nitin Agrawal

Director and Consultant Pediatric Intensivist
The Children's Hospital, Vadodara, Gujarat
nagrwal1975@yahoo.co.in

29. Dr. Pankaj Goswami

MBBS, DOMS
Ophthalmologist
Guwahati, Assam
purusuttam123@gmail.com

30. Dr. Pankaj Kohli

BDS, FETP, Senior Dental Surgeon
Uttarakhand
pkohli1220@gmail.com

31. Dr. Sanjay Maheshwari

BAMS, PGDYE, DNHE
Consultant Ayurvedic Physician
Pranav Yoga Ayurveda Healthcare.
Udaipur Rajasthan
pranavnaad@gmail.com

32. Dr. Satish Kamat

MS, DNB, FACRSI
Cancer Surgeon
MUMBAI
satishvkamat@gmail.com

33. Dr. Shubham Sabarwal

MD Psychiatry, Founder, Macflins Mindcare
Psychiatrist | Mental Health Educator | Doctorpreneur
South Dumdum, West Bengal
shubhamsabherwal2@gmail.com

34. Dr. Shubhangi Mundhada

MBBS, M.D (Obstetrics & Gynaecology)
MD Geetai Hospital, Amravati, Maharashtra
drshubhangimundhada@gmail.com

35. Dr. Sivaranjani

Dermatologist
Villupuram, Chennai
sivaderm21@gmail.com

36. Dr. S. R. Sharma

MBBS MS General Surgery
Solan, Himachal Pradesh
srsharma300@gmail.com

37. Dr. Sumana Talakokkula

MBBS, DA, DGO
Obstetrics and Gynecologist
Bengaluru
drsumana123@gmail.com

38. Dr. Suneet Sud

MBBS MS General Surgery
FMAS, DNB, MRCS-I, FIAGES, FACRSI, MNIMS, FEHS
Safal Hospital Nagpur
suneet70@yahoo.com

39. Dr. T J Pradeep Kumar

Consultant Physician, Cardio-Diabetologist,
and Critical Care Expert
Bengaluru
drpradeep@brookefieldhospital.com

40. Vaibhavi Gopashetty

CEO - Vardhan Fertility & Laparoscopy
Women's Care Center,
Bengaluru
gopashetty.vaibhavi7@gmail.com

INTRODUCTION

I Can Heal is more than just a book. It is a mirror to a quiet revolution brewing in the hearts of doctors across the country—those who chose to go beyond the stethoscope, beyond the routine, and beyond the expected.

Medicine, at its core, is not just a science. It's a calling. A journey of empathy, grit, and relentless purpose. For some, it also becomes an entrepreneurial adventure—one where healing extends not only to patients, but to the systems and communities around them.

In *I Can Heal*, you will meet doctors who dared to dream differently. They didn't just consult—they created. Some built multi-specialty hospitals from scratch, defying the odds of funding and infrastructure. Others set up specialty clinics rooted in empathy, innovation, and deep listening. A few embraced the power of digital—telemedicine, social media, and tech—to reach people beyond borders, redefining the very way healthcare is delivered.

These stories are not just about success—they are about purpose, resilience, and the courage to take bold, sometimes lonely, steps. Each chapter brings you closer to real lives, real sacrifices, and real impact. In a world where most doctors follow the traditional path; this book is a beacon for those who wonder if there's more. And if you've ever asked yourself:

- Can I start my own clinic or hospital?
- Is it possible to blend business with ethical care?
- Can I use online platforms to help more patients?
- How can I build a successful medical career?

Then this book is for you.

I Can Heal is your roadmap to transformation. A reminder that healing doesn't stop at a hospital gate—it spills into how you lead, how you serve, and how you build. Whether you're just starting your career or ready to take your practice to the next level, the insights in these pages will ignite your passion and expand your vision.

Every story is a testament to one truth:

If you have the heart to heal and the will to act, you can build something greater than yourself.

Because healing is not just what we do.

It's who we are.

Welcome to *I Can Heal*. Let the journey begin.

CHAPTER 1

HOW I STARTED AND ESTABLISHED MY HOMEOPATHIC PRACTICE IN KANPUR

Dr. Alkab Hasan Nazar,
Homeopathy practitioner,
Kanpur.

When people look at my journey today, they often see a thriving homeopathic practice and a growing online presence. But what they don't see are the challenges, the long nights, and the deep faith I had to keep in homeopathy—and myself—while building it all from scratch.

My Beginning: From Internship to Independent Practice

My journey started during my internship in Kanpur. It was then that I truly began to appreciate the power of homeopathy—not just as a science, but as a healing system that could touch lives. Even though I didn't have a well-established setup or many resources at that point, I felt a strong calling to open my own clinic.

The early days were hard. I didn't have much staff, my finances were tight, and there were moments of doubt. But what I had was passion—and I leaned into it. Slowly, I started treating patients, explaining homeopathy to them, and earning their trust one case at a time.

My Family and Educational Roots

Medicine runs deep in my family. We owned a homeopathic medical store, so I grew up surrounded by remedies, remedies, and more remedies! My brother pursued MBBS and later specialized in Nuclear Medicine, so healthcare discussions were always part of our dinner table conversations.

That atmosphere solidified my belief in the healing potential of homeopathy. I didn't choose this path just because it was familiar—it felt right. It felt like home.

Navigating Financial Struggles and Growing One Step at a Time

Starting my practice was not just a medical journey—it was a financial test too. I had to learn how to manage patient payments, deal with banks, handle day-to-day operations, and ensure that the clinic kept running. At one point, I even involved my family in supporting various aspects of the clinic.

Telemedicine was a big breakthrough. It allowed me to reach patients beyond Kanpur without needing a physical presence everywhere. Bit by bit, I started seeing growth—more patients, more word-of-mouth, and more confidence in my work.

Going Digital: The Game Changer

I realized very early that if I wanted to reach more people, I needed to show up where they were—online. So, I started posting on YouTube, Instagram, and Facebook. I wasn't trying to go viral. I just wanted to educate, share, and build a community around genuine homeopathic care.

Later, I partnered with a digital marketing agency to refine my online strategy, and that helped tremendously. More visibility led to more inquiries, and slowly, my patient base expanded beyond Kanpur. Digital platforms didn't just amplify my message—they helped build trust.

Expanding My Services: From Kanpur to Beyond

As my practice grew, I started focusing on some specific conditions—kidney stones, venereal diseases, and skin-related issues. I saw a gap in understanding and treatment in these areas, and I wanted to bridge that gap with effective homeopathic care.

Thanks to referrals, social media, and word-of-mouth, I started getting patients from nearby cities as well. I make it a point to be responsive and professional in every interaction. I believe that's key to long-term trust and success.

Educating Patients: My Responsibility

One thing that bothers me is the growing trend of self-medication, often fueled by misleading online content. I always advise patients: consult a specialist first, whether it's in Ayurveda, Homeopathy, Unani, or Allopathy.

There's a reason we study and train for years. Diagnosis and treatment need to be thoughtful—not rushed or influenced by social media trends. I see it as part of my duty to educate patients about this, both offline and online.

Staying True to Homeopathy

Many have suggested that I should mix allopathic drugs with homeopathic treatment to grow faster or cater to more patients. But I've stood firm. I don't mix systems. My belief in classical homeopathy is strong, and I stick to it. That consistency has earned me credibility, and my patients trust that what I offer is genuine and safe.

Taking It Further: Opening My Own Homeopathic Medical Store

Recently, I took another step forward—I opened a homeopathic medical store. This not only supports my offline clinic but also helps me serve patients in remote parts of India where homeopathic medicines are not easily accessible.

Through this store and my online consultations, I'm now able to extend care to areas that previously had no access to homeopathy. That, to me, feels like meaningful impact.

In Closing

My journey has taught me that with the right mindset, a willingness to learn, and a deep respect for patients, anything is possible. From a small setup in Kanpur to becoming a trusted name in homeopathy, the road hasn't been easy—but it's been worth it.

I continue to learn, grow, and evolve—not just as a doctor, but as an educator and advocate for authentic, responsible healthcare. And I hope my story inspires other young doctors to believe in themselves, even when the odds are stacked against them.

Dr. Alkab Hasan Nazar

Homeopathy practitioner
Kanpur

CHAPTER 2

THE SECRET TO RUNNING A SUCCESSFUL DENTAL PRACTICE!

Dr. Amit Patil
BDS, MDS in Maxillo-Facial Prosthodontics,
Implant Surgery & Cosmetic Dentistry, Goa

The Secret to Running a Successful Dental Practice – My Journey

If there's one thing I've learned over the years, it's that behind every healthy smile lies more than just clinical expertise. Running a successful dental practice takes vision, strategy, and a deep sense of responsibility—not just toward patients, but also towards your team, your finances, and yourself.

My name is Dr. Amit Patil, and I'm a dental professional practicing in the beautiful state of Goa. My journey in dentistry has been one of steady growth, constant learning, and balancing ambition with purpose. Today, I manage two thriving clinics, but it all started with a spark and a dream.

My Career Growth

I am a highly skilled MDS dental specialist with a strong educational foundation in dentistry. Completed my Bachelor of Dental Surgery (BDS) from the prestigious *Rajiv Gandhi University of Health Sciences (RGUHS) Bangalore*, one of the top-ranked health sciences universities in India. I further advanced my expertise by pursuing a Master of Dental Surgery (MDS) from the renowned *JSS University, Mysore* a premier institution in dental education. In the initial days I Served as Dental Officer at ECHS polyclinic: Ministry of Defense (Panjim) for 5 years. This rigorous academic training and clinical experience have equipped me with the knowledge and skills necessary to provide exceptional patient care.

With a passion for delivering personalized, gentle, and state-of-the-art dental care, I remain dedicated to helping patients achieve optimal oral health and beautiful smiles. My areas of expertise include Implant Surgery, Smile Design, Dentures, Crown & Bridge, Full Mouth Rehabilitation, Aligners, cosmetic dentistry, and Digital Dentistry. As a committed and caring dental professional, I stay up to date with the latest advancements in dentistry, ensuring that patients receive the most effective and efficient treatments available.

I am currently practising the art of Dentistry with my wife Dr. Janvi, and we have clinics at Porvorim & Mapusa

Where It All Began

My inspiration to pursue dentistry came from a personal place. I used to accompany my father for his dental appointments and watch how our family dentist treated him—not just with skill, but with genuine care. That left a lasting impression on me. I realized then how powerful a dentist's role could be in someone's life.

Clinical Skills Alone Aren't Enough

Very early on, I realized that good clinical work was just one part of the equation. Managing a dental practice was a completely different ballgame. I had to learn everything—how to budget wisely, when and where to invest, how to recruit and retain the right staff, and even how to track the return on investment (ROI) of marketing efforts.

Running a clinic meant making smart choices every single day. I had to ensure that equipment was maintained, salaries were paid on time, and patients continued to walk in—happy, satisfied, and ready to return.

Start Small, But Think Big

When I first started my own practice, I was cautious with my spending. I bought only what was absolutely necessary—a dental chair, a compressor, and a few basic tools. It wasn't glamorous, but it was enough. As my practice grew and patient expectations increased, I gradually added more advanced tech like intraoral scanners and imaging systems.

I always tell young dentists: don't get carried away with fancy equipment at the start. Grow with intention. Let your clinic evolve with your experience and patient needs.

Quality Over Quantity, Always

In our line of work, there's always a temptation to see more patients, fill more slots, and speed things up. But I've learned to value quality over quantity. I'd rather treat fewer patients with utmost care than rush through procedures just to fill the books.

Before opening my clinic, I worked in a supportive setup where I could save money, sharpen my skills, and plan carefully. That phase gave me the cushion to start on my terms—without financial stress, and with clarity about the kind of clinic I wanted to run.

Balancing Work and Family

While I love what I do, I never wanted my work to take away from my family. My evenings are sacred—I make it a point to spend quality time with my son. That's possible only because I've learned to manage my schedule, delegate responsibilities, and build a team I trust.

I've also been toying with the idea of starting a YouTube channel—something educational, something that gives back. Dental health is still misunderstood by many, and I'd love to simplify it for the public.

Money Matters and the Power of a Good Team

Running a clinic isn't just about treating teeth—it's about running a business. I keep a close eye on finances. Every rupee counts. From salaries to maintenance, from materials to marketing—every expense needs to be planned.

I also can't emphasize enough how important a good team is. The right staff can uplift the entire patient experience. Hiring is not just about skill—it's about attitude, empathy, and alignment with the clinic's vision.

Why Technology is My Best Ally

Dentistry today is evolving fast. I've integrated tools like Exocad into my practice for designing crowns, bridges, and implants. These tools allow me to scan jaws accurately, take digital impressions, and simulate outcomes for better precision and patient satisfaction.

We've also started using robotic systems for implant placement—it's been a game changer in terms of speed, precision, and patient comfort. Technology, when used right, doesn't replace us—it enhances what we do.

Doctorpreneur Academy: A Turning Point

A big turning point in my journey was joining the **Doctorpreneur Academy**. The mentorship, workshops, and community support gave me practical tools to refine my practice.

I learned better hiring strategies, smarter marketing techniques, and how to manage operations more efficiently. But most importantly, I started thinking long-term. I began building a personal brand, and looking beyond just clinic numbers—towards impact, education, and leadership.

My Advice to Aspiring Dentists

If you're just starting out, here's what I'd say:

- **Start slow.** You don't need everything on day one. Buy as you grow.
- **Gain experience.** Work in a clinic. Learn. Save. Observe.
- **Go for MDS.** Specialization opens more doors and adds credibility.
- **Stay updated.** Dentistry is changing—keep up with technology and techniques.
- **Balance your life.** You're a professional, but you're also a person. Don't forget your family, your health, your peace.

Looking Ahead: Building More Than Smiles

I'm proud of what I've built—but I know the journey isn't over. I want to create more awareness, mentor younger dentists, and maybe even expand further someday. For now, I'm focused on making every patient feel cared for, every team member feel valued, and every challenge feel like an opportunity.

I'm not just building a dental practice—I'm building a legacy.

Dr. Amit Patil BDS

MDS in Maxillo-Facial Prosthodontics,
Implant Surgery & Cosmetic Dentistry

CHAPTER 3

RUNNING A HOSPITAL IS MORE THAN JUST PROVIDING MEDICAL CARE

Dr Arjun Hosalli
MBBS, MD (Internal Medicine), FCCM
CONSULTANT PHYSICIAN & INTENSIVIST
Gangavathi, Karnataka

$\mathcal{R}$unning a hospital is not just about providing medical care—it's about leadership, strategic planning, and navigating daily challenges that extend far beyond the clinic walls. As a doctor and hospital entrepreneur, I have come to understand that the role demands resilience, foresight, and a commitment to continuous learning. With the unwavering support and guidance of the Doctorpreneur Academy, I have transformed my vision into reality by building a 30-bed, multispecialty hospital capable of handling Level four critical care cases. And now, I am gearing up for further expansion.

A Hospital Rooted in Positivity and Purpose

My journey began with a significant mindset shift. I moved away from focusing solely on operational stress to embracing positivity and purpose-driven leadership. Since 2017, my hospital has been a beacon of hope for patients requiring critical medical and surgical care. I realized early on that my role was not just to treat but to create an institution that prioritized patient care, staff well-being, and sustainable growth.

Strategic Growth from 30 to 45 Beds

Expanding a hospital is not just about adding more beds; it requires strategic staffing and planning. Currently, my team consists of:

- 4 full-time doctors
- 2 duty doctors
- 4 visiting consultants

To support our growing patient base, I am adding a pediatrician and another surgeon while increasing the bed capacity to 45. The Doctorpreneur Academy has been instrumental in helping me analyze staffing needs, optimize workflows, and implement sustainable expansion strategies.

Family Support and Financial Planning

Behind every successful doctorpreneur is a strong support system. For me, my visionary parents provided not only emotional encouragement but also essential financial planning. My mother's care, patience, and strength were invaluable in helping me navigate the intense physical and mental demands of establishing a hospital. Through the Doctorpreneur Academy, I learned how to structure my finances, scale my hospital without compromising on quality, and balance my professional and personal life effectively.

Mastering Space and Systems in a Congested Setup

Building a hospital in a limited space comes with unique challenges. Every square foot must be optimized to ensure maximum efficiency. I went through multiple layout iterations before finalizing a design that worked. Some key lessons I learned:

- Every square foot matters.
- Delegation is non-negotiable.
- A successful hospital is built with strong teamwork.

By implementing efficient systems and space management techniques, I created a highly functional setup despite spatial constraints.

Delegation and Personalized HR Management

One of the most crucial skills I developed was the art of delegation. I had to shift from doing everything myself to trusting my team and managing staff with a people-first approach. I learned to communicate with each employee based on their individual interests and strengths, which helped me:

- Maintain staff morale.
- Reduce attrition.
- Build a motivated and loyal healthcare team.

Through The Doctorpreneur Academy, I received training in HR management, team engagement, and leadership communication, all of which transformed me from a clinician into a confident hospital administrator.

People Over Processes: Managing Staff with Empathy

Rather than reacting negatively to staff mistakes, I chose to focus on:

- Recognizing small wins.
- Acknowledging staff contributions.
- Encouraging accountability with kindness.

This empathetic approach has fostered a supportive hospital culture, aligned with my core belief: "Grow your practice by growing your people."

Patient Behavior and Systemic Realities in Indian Healthcare

One of the biggest challenges I face is the conservative patient mindset, where people often prioritize symptomatic relief over comprehensive treatment. Additionally, systemic constraints such as ICU closures for infection control are frequently misunderstood by patients. Through The Doctorpreneur Academy, I learned how to communicate effectively, educate patients, and maintain transparency while addressing system limitations.

Staying Local: Growth with Roots

Choosing to build my hospital in my hometown has been incredibly fulfilling. The deep connection with my community allows me to serve people who need quality healthcare the most. This localized approach has strengthened doctor-patient relationships, built long-term trust, and contributed to both personal and community growth.

Fostering Collaboration Over Competition

Doctors must collaborate, not compete. Despite improvements in the doctor-patient ratio, healthcare gaps still exist, especially in North India. I firmly believe that by building collaborative networks, doctors can serve patients more efficiently, support each other, and expand care access in smaller towns. The Doctorpreneur Academy actively promotes this spirit of unity by fostering shared learning, joint ventures, and professional networking.

Guiding Others Through Resources and Webinars

I am passionate about helping other doctors navigate the complexities of hospital ownership and management. I share resources, tools, and webinar links to support fellow doctorpreneurs. My advice to aspiring hospital owners: Invest in your mindset, seek structured training, and commit to continuous learning—starting with The Doctorpreneur Academy, which provided me with clarity, confidence, and a roadmap for success.

Conclusion: A Hospital Built on Heart and Strategy

My hospital is more than just a building; it is a vision brought to life through leadership, strategic planning, and deep community care. With the right mindset, structured learning, and a committed team, I have created a model that blends modern medicine with a human touch.

For doctors who dream of building their own hospitals, my journey proves that with purpose, planning, and the right mentorship, you can create healthcare spaces that truly make a difference.

Dr Arjun Hosalli
General Physician and Intensive Care Specialist
Gangavathi, Karnataka

CHAPTER 4

HOW ACUPRESSURE CHANGED LIVES – MY JOURNEY OF HEALING FROM THE HEART

Ashvini Atre Kulkarni
Acupressure Expert and Licensed
Acupuncturist by certification
Pune

*I*f someone had told me years ago that I would leave behind 'machines and blueprints' for 'healing touch' and 'breathwork', I would've smiled in disbelief. But today, as I look back, I realize that life had a greater plan— one that led me from being 'the only female mechanical engineering student in my batch' to becoming 'a healer', who now blends ....

- Western Modern Medical Science and Eastern philosophy ,
- Cyclic energy patterns in human body and Laws of Universe
- Tripodic connectivity of Body, Mind and Soul,
- 'Marm Bindus' and 'Tridoshas' mentioned in Ayurveda
- And overall simplicity in application while eradicating pains and ultimately root cause of diseases.

The Turning Point

I didn't choose healing. Healing chose me.

I started my career in Mechanical engineering— machine drawings, flowcharts, power engineering and mechanics, with 'precision, logic, and numbers'. I loved handling different types of machines, understanding the sequence of operations, fault-finding--- in the total system or in individual units or parts. I was running a business related to 'Mechanical Engineering Design Services'.

The most colorful feather in the crown was:"The Best Woman Entrepreneur" (From all over Maharashtra and Goa), '"Maharashtra Udyogini" '- Award in 2010, and prestigious ISB scholarship under Goldman Sacs program, thereafter.

But when health challenges entered my personal life, I began questioning everything. Traditional medicine gave me answers, yes—but not all of them. Something was missing. That "something" became my quest.

In 2014, I stumbled upon Brahma Vidhya, an ancient Indian discipline rooted in breath and mental energy. The moment I experienced it, I knew—I had found something profound. I wasn't just learning; I was healing. And that healing extended to others, organically.

From infinite to finite, from metaphysical to physical, from cosmic structures to tiny human cells………. Energy , Energy and Energy… only the forms are different.

From Pain to Purpose

People often ask me, "Why acupressure?"

Because it works ---- with energy, for energy, by energy.

Because it's a divine therapy ---- uses inbuilt mechanisms and internal energy to cure.

Because it balances ----- interlinked human body systems.

Because it predicts ---- failure in the organ / system much earlier.

Because it is ---- inexpensive and without any side effects.

Because I saw pain reduce, surgeries avoided, and smiles return.

Previously I handled machines.. having no emotions ….

And now.. I take care of machines having emotions..

with emotions… and… for emotions….!!!

The Science of Simplicity

Healing doesn't have to be complicated. With the right diagnosis and the right application of -- just pressure / seeds /magnets / colors on acupoints of hands and feet, your body can reset itself. I've seen patients bounce back from Chronic Fatigue, Arthritis, Coronary Artery Disease, Sciatica, Paralysis, even near-stroke conditions—all through mindful, consistent acupressure. And now I say .. I am into 'Re-engineering of Human Health'.

One of the most moving stories was of a child born with no sensation in one leg. His parents came in, desperate and heartbroken. After months of work, that child started walking, running, and eventually playing like other kids. That one smile was worth every ounce of effort.

I received the Maharashtra Udyogini' award again —but the real award was the joy in that mother's eyes, unmatched by any other global award.

During the pandemic, when medical help was inaccessible to many, I relied on acupressure. Each patient received a unique protocol. Methi seeds, dried peas, or tiny magnets—these became tools of transformation. One patient at a time, one healing at a time, we made it through.

Healing the Whole Family

As I treated patients, I realized: illness rarely affects just one person. When someone is unwell, the whole family hurts. I began focusing not just on physical recovery but also emotional and energetic wellness—for caregivers, too.

That's why my sessions are never rushed. I spend nearly two hours with each patient. I go deep into their story, asking about their lifestyle, habits, emotions, even sleep patterns, including dreams. It's only then that the root of illness begins to reveal itself.

Remarkable Mile stone

The effects of acupressure treatment increased multi-fold after I began practicing 'Brahmvidhya Techniques – (Spiritual Breathing exercises and Meditation)' on a higher and higher scale. Personally, it was like. I was getting Award after Award, seeing transformation in results of the fusion of Acupressure and Brahmvidhya. As nearly every case thereafter resulted in enhanced healing and joy and satisfaction in patients' remarkable recovery post 2020.

And then another precious feather was added to my crown ... 'Brahmvidya Teacher'.

Beyond Borders, Beyond Hospitals

Today, through digital platforms, I work with patients across the globe, with just one clinic having an energetic ambience. No hospital setup. No surgical tools. Just knowledge, Brahmavidhya teachings, and connection to cosmic energy.

Acupressure, I've found, is not bound by geography. It's universal, safe, and deeply personal.

One major gap I noticed, though, was in how alternative therapies were being taught, scattered information, confusing videos, and no clear structure. That's where AI and curated learning platforms come in.

I dream of creating a centralized hub—a clean, efficient, compassionate space—for healing education. The world needs it.

Why More Doctors Should Explore This

I often meet doctors who are curious but hesitant. "Will it work? Isn't it too different from what we learned?"

My answer is simple— experience it.

Human Anatomy and Physiology is the same for mankind. The difference is in the approach to treatment. Hence, many 'pathies' exist. Acupressure is a holistic medicine. But to showcase evidence to the modern world, all Acu points on the human body were tested by Dr. Voll of Germany with the physical instrument called 'Darmetron'. So, just change your 'brain specs ', apply it and see transformation.

This isn't about replacing Allopathy / Homeopathy etc. It's about enhancing care, reducing costs, and bringing back human touch into medicine. Acupressure isn't magic—it's proven and accepted 'energy based science', and my intention is cohesive.

Young doctors especially need to understand the power of each organ's internal energy flow, its connectivity with other organs, systems, endocrine glands, tissues and even to cells. This isn't a soft skill—it's a core skill for tomorrow's healthcare.

The Doctorpreneur Academy Shift

Joining the Doctorpreneur Academy was like finding my tribe. I was no longer just a healer—I became a structured thinker, a confident communicator, and an educator with impact.

Through the academy, I learned how to:

- Convert my years of knowledge into digestible, digital courses
- Use social media and online tools to spread awareness
- Build a brand rooted in compassion and clarity
- Engage with patients beyond the clinic
- Lead with purpose, not just practice

Now, my mission is scalable. What started in one room in Pune, is now reaching living rooms across continents.

Healing Is a Journey—Not a Prescription

If I've learned anything, it's this—healing isn't about pills or points. It's about blissful presence. And the eternal purpose of our existence is 'Victorious Living' and to achieve 'Ultimate Pleasure' and lastly.... 'Enlightenment'...!!!!

It's about believing that your body, as well as mind want to heal—and sometimes, all it needs is a nudge in the right direction.

Whether it's a seed on your palm, color dots on fingers, a breath held a few seconds longer, or a right thought—transformation is possible.

I'm **Ashvini Atre Kulkarni**.

- Mechanical Engineer and a successful woman entrepreneur by recognition,
- Licensed Acupuncturist by certification. 4 years of training
- Renowned Acupressurist by Calling.
- A believer that even the simplest tools, like tiny stones/ pebbles can create the most profound changes.

And hence 'Appointed Healer' by the celestial empire.

Let us work together to enhance human lives to a higher state of existence.

Lastly, this is not just my story. It's our story. One that's just getting started.

CHAPTER 5

INITIAL STRUGGLES TO SUCCESS: JOURNEY OF ALL DENTISTS

Dr. Atindra Das
Dental Surgeon & tobacco cessation expert
Jagiroad, Assam

Crafting a Vision-Driven Practice

I believe that every dental practice should begin with a clear vision and mission. When I started my journey, I relied solely on my clinical skills and intuition. However, after joining the Doctorpreneur Academy in 2021, I developed a structured framework to align my clinic's goals with patient outcomes. This shift allowed me to refine my mission—not just to treat, but to create, a lasting impact.

Through strategic mentorship, I learned how to scale my operations efficiently and lead my practice with clarity. What began as a modest setup has now transformed into a well-structured centre for reliable and responsive dental care, making a significant difference in my hometown.

Enhancing Access and Efficiency in Local Dental Care

When I started, I faced significant challenges, including limited resources, expensive dental tools, and long patient wait times. With guidance from The Doctorpreneur Academy, I implemented efficient systems, hired additional support staff, and streamlined patient management. These changes led to:

- Significantly reduced patient wait times
- Expansion from a single dental chair to four fully equipped chairs
- Enhanced workflow and higher patient satisfaction

By making these strategic improvements, I transformed my practice into a centre that provides accessible, quality dental care in a community that previously had limited options.

A Legacy of Service Inspired by Family

My commitment to dentistry is deeply rooted in my family values. My father, a source of immense inspiration, passed away in 2010. Driven by his legacy, my brother and I now run our practice together, ensuring that our work is not just about treating patients, but also about uplifting the community.

This strong sense of familial duty fuels my dedication to serving the region with compassion, integrity, and professionalism.

Mentorship and Digital Marketing: Game Changers in Dentistry

A major turning point in my journey was the introduction of mentorship and digital marketing strategies through The Doctorpreneur Academy. I realized that traditional word-of-mouth marketing was not enough in today's digital era. By leveraging digital tools, I:

- Expanded my patient reach through engaging video content
- Educated the community on dental hygiene and procedures
- Built trust and credibility through consistent online engagement

What was once an underutilized marketing tool became a powerful driver of growth, enabling me to establish a strong digital presence and attract more patients.

Morning Rituals: Balancing the Dentist and the Human

Beyond dentistry, I follow a unique morning ritual routine—a practice encouraged by The Doctorpreneur Academy. These daily rituals include meditation, affirmations, and self-reflection, helping me maintain balance in both my personal and professional life.

My routine focuses on five key life pillars:

- Self – Personal growth and well-being
- Health – Physical and mental fitness
- Income – Financial stability and growth
- Family – Strengthening relationships and support systems
- Team – Building a motivated and aligned workforce

By prioritizing these aspects, I ensure that my success as a dentist does not come at the cost of personal well-being.

Guiding Young Dentists: Strategy, Mindset, and Affordability

I am passionate about mentoring young dentists, especially those just starting out. Through insights gained at the Doctorpreneur Academy, I share key lessons on setting up a successful practice. I emphasize that rural setups can be more affordable than most assume, with basic equipment costs starting from ₹3–4 lakhs. More importantly, I highlight that:

- Success is not just about location, but about mindset and mentorship.
- Persistence and proper planning are more powerful than financial resources.
- A well-structured, long-term approach is key to sustainability.

By sharing these insights, I encourage new practitioners to stay resilient, think strategically, and seek the right guidance.

Making a Difference: Stories that Inspire

Among the many lives I have impacted, one case remains particularly memorable—a 9-year-old boy who lost a front tooth. Acting swiftly, I replanted the tooth, restoring the child's smile and confidence.

This is just one of many instances where my expertise, quick decision-making, and dedication have profoundly changed lives.

Serving Communities Beyond the Clinic

For me, dentistry extends beyond the walls of my clinic. I actively organize dental camps in villages within a 20-kilometer radius, ensuring that quality dental care reaches underserved communities. These camps focus on:

- Providing free dental check-ups and consultations
- Educating villagers on the importance of oral hygiene
- Bridging the gap in healthcare accessibility

Guided by The Doctorpreneur Academy's principle of service-driven entrepreneurship, I remain committed to making a difference beyond my practice.

Conclusion: A Dental Trailblazer with a Mentor's Mindset

I see myself as more than just a dentist—I am a visionary, mentor, and community leader. My journey proves that with the right guidance, strategy, and dedication, a small-town practitioner can create an immense impact.

From expanding rural dental access to mastering digital marketing, I demonstrate that success is not just about skill but about heart, vision, and action. Through my work, I continue to inspire, uplift, and redefine dentistry—not just as a profession, but as a mission.

Dr. Atindra Das
Dentist
Jagiroad, Assam

CHAPTER 6

THE HEARTBEAT OF CHANGE: MY JOURNEY FROM FARMLAND TO CARDIOLOGY

Dr Birendra Kumar
MBBS MD DM Cardiologist
Bhagalpur, Bihar

Growing up in a small farming village near Bhagalpur, Bihar, I never imagined that one day I would become a cardiologist. My childhood was spent in the vast fields, where the rhythm of life was dictated by the seasons and the toil of my parents. With no family background in medicine, my dream of becoming a doctor seemed distant, if not impossible. Yet, an unwavering curiosity and a deep-seated desire to serve my community pushed me forward.

From Farmer's Son to Renowned Cardiologist

My journey into medicine began with relentless dedication and hard work. I secured admission to King George's Medical College (KGMC), one of India's most esteemed institutions. The rigorous training and exposure to advanced cardiology refined my skills and strengthened my resolve. While many of my peers pursued careers in metropolitan hospitals, I knew my true calling lay elsewhere—back home, where healthcare was still a distant luxury for many.

Overcoming Challenges

Returning to Bhagalpur was a decision driven by purpose, but it was not without challenges. I quickly realized that rural healthcare was plagued by issues far beyond medical treatment: lack of awareness, inadequate facilities, and deeply ingrained superstitions made it difficult for people to trust modern medicine.

Determined to address these issues, I started conducting weekend clinics in nearby villages. I listened to my patients' concerns, educated them about heart health, and slowly built their confidence in medical science. However, I knew that good intentions alone wouldn't be enough—I needed a sustainable model to make quality healthcare accessible to the masses.

Building a Healthcare Ecosystem

To bridge the gap between vision and reality, I sought mentorship from the Doctorpreneur Academy. This platform gave me valuable insights into the business and operational aspects of healthcare—statutory requirements, vendor negotiations, fire safety compliance, and marketing strategies. Armed with this knowledge, I laid the foundation for my own clinic.

Starting with a modest setup, I focused on a holistic approach to healthcare. I organized regular health camps, providing free check-ups, and consultations to build trust within the community. Recognizing the difficulties patients faced in traveling to a hospital, I leveraged telemedicine, ensuring timely medical intervention even in remote areas.

But I wanted to do more than just treat patients—I wanted to empower them. I trained village health workers to act as first responders in medical emergencies. By collaborating with community leaders, I reinforced the idea that healthcare was not just a service, but a collective responsibility.

Success Mantra: Grit, Determination, and Community Engagement

My journey wasn't just about setting up a clinic—it was about transforming an entire ecosystem. I engaged directly with my people, listened to their fears, and provided care with empathy. This approach not only helped me build a strong practice but also inspired young minds in the region to consider careers in medicine.

Slowly but surely, my efforts started yielding results. More healthcare initiatives were introduced in the area, strengthening the medical infrastructure and making quality healthcare more accessible. The ripple effect of my work was evident in the growing trust of the community and the improved health awareness among the people.

A Legacy of Hope and Health

Looking back, my journey from being a farmer's son to a cardiologist serving my own community has been nothing short of transformative. It has been a journey of resilience, learning, and an unwavering belief in the power of healthcare to change lives.

I continue to push forward, striving to expand my reach and enhance the quality of care available to my people. My story is not just mine—it belongs to every doctor who chooses to serve where they are needed the most. It is a testament to the fact that with passion, persistence, and a commitment to service, even the most formidable challenges can be turned into opportunities for progress.

As I move ahead, my mission remains clear—to build a healthcare system that is inclusive, accessible, and driven by the needs of the people. The heartbeat of change has begun, and I am honored to be a part of it.

Dr Birendra Kumar
Cardiologist
Bhagalpur, Bihar

CHAPTER 7

STRUGGLES, STRENGTH & SUCCESS – MY LIFE-CHANGING STORY

Dr Chitra Patil
BAMS
Ayurveda and QuantumHealing Expert
Bengaluru, Karnataka

My Journey of Healing, Strength, and Purpose

Life often throws unexpected challenges our way, but I have always believed that struggles can be transformed into something meaningful. As a BAMS doctor specializing in yoga therapy and quantum healing, my journey has been shaped by both adversity and resilience. Facing major health setbacks, including open-heart surgery, I refused to surrender. Instead, I turned my pain into power, dedicating my life to helping others heal through holistic wellness.

A Journey of Strength and Resilience

My path has been anything but easy. Battling serious health conditions, I had to find the courage to fight back and rebuild my life. My journey exemplifies how determination and resilience can help us overcome even the toughest obstacles.

- Fighting Against All Odds: Instead of letting my health struggles define me, I used them as motivation to learn, grow, and evolve.
- Breaking Barriers as a Woman in Medicine: I carved a unique path in holistic wellness, proving that passion and dedication can overcome any barrier.
- Finding Purpose Through Struggles: My personal experiences gave me a deep understanding of healing beyond conventional medicine, leading me to explore yoga therapy and quantum healing.

Healing Through Holistic Wellness

I firmly believe in the power of natural healing. Integrating yoga therapy and quantum healing, I help individuals achieve overall well-being—physically, mentally, and emotionally. My approach is not just about treating symptoms, but about promoting sustainable health and happiness.

- Yoga Therapy: Enhances physical strength, flexibility, and mental clarity.
- Quantum Healing: Focuses on energy balance and self-healing techniques, fostering deep healing from within.

Through my work, I teach people that true healing comes from within and that a balanced lifestyle is key to long-term wellness.

The Power of Family & Community in Healthcare

My journey would not have been possible without the unwavering support of my family. They stood by my side through personal and professional challenges, empowering me to pursue my passion for healing. However, my transformation didn't stop there.

A pivotal turning point in my career was my association with The Doctorpreneur Academy. This platform encouraged me to think beyond traditional medical boundaries and explore new possibilities in healthcare. Through structured mentorship, I gained the confidence to take bold steps and apply my expertise in innovative ways.

I extend my heartfelt gratitude to Dr. Amit Moga and Dr. Pranav Sharma, whose guidance has helped me push past limitations and explore new avenues in medico-entrepreneurship, digital health, and holistic wellness. Their mentorship has inspired me to break barriers, adopt a growth mindset, and make a greater impact in the world of healthcare.

An Inspiration for Healthcare Professionals

My story is not just about overcoming personal struggles—it is about using those struggles to serve others. As healthcare workers, we often prioritize our patients while neglecting our well-being. My journey serves as a powerful reminder to:

- Take care of ourselves while caring for others.
- Embrace holistic approaches in healthcare.
- Find strength in challenges and keep moving forward.

My life-changing journey is a testament to the power of resilience, holistic healing, and the courage to embrace change. I hope my story inspires others to learn, grow, and make a meaningful impact in the world of healthcare.

Dr Chitra Patil

Ayurveda and Quantum Healing Expert
Bengaluru, Karnataka.

CHAPTER 8

MY RAPID CAREER RISE IN OPHTHALMOLOGY – A JOURNEY OF VISION AND GROWTH

Dr Devanshi Shah
MS, Gold Medalist, DNB FNERF (Oculoplasty) FRCS UK.
Ophthalmologist
Mumbai

*I*n the bustling city of Mumbai, amidst towering skyscrapers and the relentless energy of life, I found my calling in ophthalmology. The journey to building Deevine Eye Care & Multispecialty Centre was not an impulsive decision but the resulted from years of training, resilience, and an unwavering vision. Every step I took brought me closer to my dream—to transform lives by restoring eyesight and providing exceptional eye care.

A Dream Years in the Making

My path in ophthalmology began with years of rigorous study and hands-on experience. After completing my MS from Saurashtra University with a Gold Medal and pursuing a prestigious fellowship at one of the world's leading hospitals, I was equipped with knowledge, skill, and an insatiable drive to make a difference.

Through these years, I encountered the many challenges of the medical profession—long hours, emotional toll, and the constant evolution of technology. But through it all, I held onto my dream, knowing that one day, I would establish a centre where patients felt seen, heard, and cared for beyond just their medical needs.

The Academy That Fueled My Journey

While medical expertise formed my foundation, I soon realised that building a successful private practice required more than just clinical skills. That's when I joined The Doctorpreneur Academy—not just as a student but as someone eager to turn aspirations into reality.

The academy became my accountability partner, providing structured financial planning, branding, and patient engagement guidance. It gave me access to mentors, industry experts, and a community of like-minded doctors who propelled me forward. With every resource I accessed and every strategy I implemented, I could feel my dream turning into a tangible success.

Finding My "Why"

At the core of my journey was a deep and powerful "why." I didn't just want to perform eye surgeries or run a practice—I wanted to empower patients with awareness, provide accessible eye care, and contribute meaningfully to the healthcare ecosystem. This purpose kept me grounded and gave me the strength to push through challenges.

Every time I helped restore someone's vision, I felt the profound impact of my work. To me, ophthalmology was more than a profession; it was a mission to bring "divine vision" to those in need.

A Shift in Mindset

Success in healthcare isn't just about technical expertise—it's about adopting the right mindset. I learned to view challenges as opportunities, failures as stepping stones, and limitations as temporary obstacles. Instead of fearing the complexities of private practice, I embraced them with innovation, resilience, and adaptability.

By shifting my perspective, I positioned myself ahead in an ever-evolving healthcare landscape. I no longer saw my journey as just running a clinic; I saw it as building an impactful legacy.

Creating My Unique Identity

Differentiation is the key to building a successful practice. I built my brand not just on technical excellence but on patient-centred care and cutting-edge technology.

My motto became simple: "Listen to your patients and always go the extra mile." This philosophy shaped my practice, earning the trust of my patients and setting me apart from others in the field.

By consistently innovating and adapting my services to patient needs, I established myself as a trusted name in ophthalmology—someone known not just for expertise but for empathy and personalised care.

Understanding My Target Audience

Running a successful private practice is more than just medicine—it's about understanding the people you serve. I spent time analysing my ideal patient demographic, their needs, fears, and expectations.

This understanding allowed me to refine my services, marketing strategies, and patient interactions in a way that truly resonated with my community. It wasn't just about treating eye conditions; it was about creating an experience where patients felt valued and cared for.

Harnessing the Power of Social Media

Recognising the influence of digital platforms, I turned to social media to broaden my reach. Platforms like Instagram and LinkedIn became powerful tools to educate, engage, and connect with a wider audience.

On Instagram, (@eyecarewithdrdee), I started sharing informative reels, answering common eye health questions, and hosting live Q&A sessions. This strategy not only helped me build trust with existing patients but also positioned me as a thought leader in ophthalmology.

Through patient testimonials and interactive content, I strengthened my credibility and attracted new patients who were seeking expert care with a personal touch.

Giving Back: Building a Legacy through Charity

Beyond professional success, I felt a deep responsibility to give back to the community. I took steps to establish a charitable initiative focused on providing affordable eye care to underprivileged communities.

Through outreach programs and eye camps, I ensured that vision care was accessible to those who needed it the most. Recently, I was honored by the Minister of Public Health and Family Welfare for my contributions,performing over 200 cataract surgeries under the Roshni Cataract Service program at Lilavati Hospital, Mumbai.

This recognition was not just an award but a reminder of my purpose—to serve, heal, and make a lasting impact.

A Beacon of Hope in Healthcare

Looking back, my journey as an Ophthalmologist has been one of resilience, learning, and unwavering commitment. Every challenge I faced became a stepping stone, and every patient I treated reaffirmed my belief in the power of compassionate healthcare.

My story is a testament that success isn't about waiting for the perfect conditions—it's about creating them. With courage, passion, and a commitment to lifelong learning, anyone can build a thriving practice while making a real difference.

As I continue to innovate, grow, and inspire, I hope my journey serves as a guiding light for aspiring doctors. Because true success isn't just about achieving milestones—it's about creating impact, one patient at a time.

Dr Devanshi Shah

Opthalmologist
Mumbai

CHAPTER 9

HOW TO START AND GROW A HOSPITAL SUCCESSFULLY.

Dr. Dilip Gupta
MBBS, MS Orthopedics
Basti, UP

From 10 Beds to a Healthcare Vision: My Journey as Dr. Dilip Gupta

In the ever-evolving world of healthcare, my journey from a modest 10-bed setup to a 50-bed and now a soon-to-be 300-bed hospital in Basti, Uttar Pradesh, has been nothing short of transformational. As a doctor, leader, and entrepreneur, I've faced my share of challenges, but each step has been deeply purposeful, guided by a commitment to serve and grow with my community.

Proactive Problem-Solving: My Core Philosophy

One thing I've always believed in is anticipating problems before they arise. Whether it's staffing, logistics, or patient flow, being proactive saves time, energy, and unnecessary stress. I've learned to respond quickly and implement solutions without delay, ensuring that our hospital operations stay smooth and focused on patient care.

From Government Service to Hospital Ownership

I began my career in government healthcare, learning the ropes in public service and understanding the depth of patient needs. But there was always a voice inside me nudging me toward creating something of my own—something sustainable, scalable, and impactful. That's how my hospital journey began. What started as a small 10-bed clinic has grown into a thriving 50-bed facility, and we are now preparing to expand to 300 beds. This vision gives me purpose every single day.

Mentorship and Social Work: Catalysts in My Journey

Social engagement and mentorship have been vital to my evolution. Early on, I leaned into community work and professional networks to build my presence and learn the business side of medicine. I can say with full confidence that mentors helped me identify blind spots I didn't even know I had. Their guidance helped me make smoother transitions and better decisions.

Staying Focused: The Power of the Right Circle

I've learned that clarity and focus come from surrounding yourself with the right people. Shifting from a government mindset to an entrepreneurial one wasn't easy, but staying true to my goals and keeping successful mentors close helped me evolve faster. Every challenge became more manageable when I had a trusted circle to fall back on.

Relocating to Basti: A Test of Faith and Endurance

When I moved from Ayodhya to Basti, I knew it wouldn't be easy. Building trust in a new town was challenging. But I kept showing up, with service, consistency, and integrity. Eventually, people noticed. But this phase also came with an intense workload and personal sacrifices, and it took a toll on my health. That's when I realized I needed to care for myself if I wanted to keep caring for others.

Balancing Identities: Beyond the Doctor's Coat

Being a doctor isn't my only identity. Yoga, meditation, and time with my family have helped me realign. I now see self-care not as a luxury, but as a necessity. When I'm centered, I make better decisions, for my patients, my team, and my future.

Professional Networks: My SIM Card Analogy

I often say a doctor without a network is like a phone without a SIM card—no matter how advanced the device, it's of little use without a connection. My network of peers, mentors, and professionals keeps me updated, supported, and inspired.

Learning Never Stops

I'm proud to say that I'm still a student. I regularly seek help and attend workshops to learn how to better manage hospital operations, delegate effectively, and reduce daily stress. Recognizing my limitations has never held me back—it's helped me grow stronger and smarter.

Family: My True Backbone

My wife is my biggest supporter. She left a prestigious government job to stand beside me in this mission. Her qualifications, sacrifices, and belief in our shared dream have been instrumental in everything we've achieved. Family, for me, is the foundation of success.

Why Small Towns Hold Big Opportunities

I've seen firsthand how smaller towns offer massive untapped potential. Less competition and more demand make it fertile ground for meaningful healthcare ventures. By focusing on quality, accessibility, and affordability, we've carved a strong identity in Basti.

Introducing Pain Management: A Strategic Win

Launching pain management services—especially for arthritis—has made a significant impact. Not only are we addressing a pressing local need, but it's also added a revenue stream that sustains other parts of the hospital. It's a win-win—for patients and the institution.

Staff Motivation: The Culture of Care

With over 60 team members, I've learned the value of investing in people. Fixed salaries, performance incentives, birthday celebrations—we do it all. A happy, motivated staff delivers better care, and I never take them for granted.

Community Collaboration: Going Beyond the Walls

I regularly organize camps, offer discounts, and engage in social media awareness campaigns. We've partnered with local groups to reach more people and build trust. For me, community engagement is as important as clinical expertise.

Branding for Doctors: A Non-Negotiable

I tell every young doctor, your brand matters. Patients trust what they see and hear consistently. A strong personal and hospital brand lets you build credibility, attract patients, and eventually delegate more confidently, giving you the freedom to grow.

Running a Hospital like a Business

One of the biggest lessons I've learned is that you have to run a hospital like a business. It doesn't mean compromising on ethics—it means building systems, teams, communication channels, and marketing strategies that work like a well-oiled machine. Only then can you offer consistent care at scale.

Doctorpreneur Academy: My Turning Point

Joining the Doctorpreneur Academy changed the game for me. I gained:

- Systems to reduce hospital errors
- Clarity on branding and team dynamics
- Mentorship and a community that truly understands doctors
- Tools to delegate, scale, and innovate with confidence
- And most importantly—vision

Through webinars, mentorship calls, and practical templates, I've become more structured and future-ready. This academy didn't just grow my hospital—it transformed *me*.

In Conclusion: Purpose, People, Progress

My journey—from government service to building a hospital empire in Basti—is proof that with purpose, the right people, and a hunger to learn, anything is possible. I'm not just building a hospital; I'm building a legacy of compassionate, community-first healthcare. And I truly believe—this is just the beginning.

Dr. Dilip Gupta

MS Orthopedics
Basti, UP

CHAPTER 10

FROM SMALL-TOWN SURGEON TO HEALTHCARE LEADER!

Dr. Dinesh Sharma
MBBS MS ORTHO
Orthopedic Surgeon
Haryana

*W*hen I look back at my journey, I see a path filled with challenges, determination, and unwavering belief in my vision. I didn't come from a privileged background, nor did I have a financial safety net when I started. But what I did have was a deep desire to bring quality orthopedic care to places where it was scarce. Today, as I stand at the helm of a thriving orthopedic hospital in Narnaul, I realize that every struggle along the way was preparing me for this moment.

A Dream Born from Challenges

My journey into medicine wasn't smooth. Getting into medical school itself was an uphill battle. I faced financial constraints, but I never let them define my future. Through sheer persistence, I ranked third in my MBBS class—proof that hard work and dedication can turn even the toughest situations into victories.

But excelling academically was just the beginning. The real challenge came when I stepped into the world of medical practice. How would I establish myself? Where would I find the right opportunities? Many of my peers were drawn to big cities, but I saw potential where others didn't— in small towns.

Finding Opportunity in Small Towns

While many doctors believe that success is only found in metro cities, I realised early on that small towns offered something equally valuable: a loyal patient base, less competition, and the chance to make a real difference. Instead of joining the crowd, I returned to my hometown, Narnaul, determined to bring advanced orthopaedic care to a region that needed it.

Starting with limited resources, I focused on building trust within the community. Slowly but surely, my practice grew. Today, that small clinic has transformed into a well-equipped orthopaedic centre, and the impact we've made on people's lives keeps me motivated every single day.

Key Lessons from My Journey

1. Start Practising Early – You Don't Need to Know Everything

Many young doctors hesitate to start their practice, thinking they need to be "fully ready." I believe this mindset only delays progress. Experience is the best teacher. The sooner you start treating patients, the sooner you gain confidence and expertise.

2. Challenges Lead to Unexpected Success

Early struggles were difficult, but they built my resilience. Every setback taught me something valuable. I learned that financial constraints, resource limitations, and self-doubt are temporary—but the lessons they teach last forever.

3. Managing a Hospital is Different from Practising Medicine

As my practice grew, I realized that running a hospital wasn't just about medical skills—it required leadership, financial planning, and management expertise. I had to understand patient engagement, staff retention, and sustainable business strategies to ensure long-term success.

4. The Role of Technology and Digital Transformation

With increasing competition in healthcare, I knew I had to embrace digital tools to stay ahead. Integrating electronic medical records, offering online consultations, and using social media marketing helped me expand my reach and streamline operations. In today's world, digital transformation isn't optional—it's essential.

5. The Importance of Staff and Team Building

A hospital is only as strong as its team. I make it a point to invest in my staff—training them, ensuring job satisfaction, and fostering a culture of teamwork. Treating my team like family has resulted in long-term stability and better patient care.

6. Growth Happens Outside Your Comfort Zone

Inspired by the Doctorpreneur Academy, I realized that true growth comes from pushing past limitations. Expanding my practice, introducing specialized treatments, and learning about hospital management were all steps outside my comfort zone—but they were necessary for transformation.

Doctorpreneur Academy: A Game Changer

The Doctorpreneur Academy played a crucial role in my journey. It taught me how to think beyond clinical practice and embrace entrepreneurship. Through this platform, I gained:

- ✓ Business and management skills to run a successful hospital
- ✓ Digital strategies to enhance patient engagement
- ✓ Marketing techniques to grow my practice
- ✓ Financial planning insights for long-term stability

Final Thoughts

My journey from financial struggles to leading a successful orthopaedic hospital is proof that success isn't about where you start—it's about how determined you are to grow. Small towns hold immense opportunities, and with the right mindset, skills, and continuous learning, doctors can create lasting impacts in healthcare.

To all my fellow doctors dreaming of building something meaningful: don't wait for the perfect moment. Start now. Push through the challenges. Learn continuously. And most importantly, believe in your vision. If I could do it, so can you.

Dr. Dinesh Sharma

Orthopedic Surgeon, Haryana

CHAPTER 11

DOCTORS, READ THIS REAL STORY BEFORE YOU START YOUR OWN HOSPITAL!

Dr.Gangambika
Gynecologist
Talikoti, Karnataka

From Struggles to Success in Healthcare: My Journey

I have always dreamed of making a difference in women's healthcare. As a gynecologist working in government hospitals, I witnessed firsthand the challenges patients faced due to limited facilities. I knew I had to do something bigger—something that would bring quality healthcare closer to the people who needed it the most.

But transforming a dream into reality is never easy. My journey from a government doctor to the founder of a 100-bed hospital was filled with challenges, missteps, and invaluable lessons that every aspiring doctorpreneur can learn from.

The Biggest Challenge: Building a Hospital from Scratch

Starting a hospital is more than just practising medicine. It requires vision, planning, financial acumen, and the ability to manage people. When I decided to build my hospital, I started with a modest plan—a 50-bed facility with minimal staff. But as I delved deeper, I realized the immense potential and growing demand for quality healthcare in my region.

I took a bold step, expanding my vision to a 100-bed multi-specialty hospital. However, this decision came with unexpected hurdles. Poor planning, unexpected delays, and financial strain almost derailed my dream.

Why Poor Planning Delayed My Hospital Project

One of the biggest mistakes I made early on was hiring the wrong team for construction. Initially, I chose local contractors, assuming they would be cost-effective and reliable. Unfortunately, they lacked experience in hospital construction, leading to several setbacks. The project faced delays due to inefficiency, and I had to change contractors twice, causing further disruptions. Design flaws and poor execution forced expensive corrections, increasing both costs and frustration.

I didn't listen to expert advice in the beginning. I thought any contractor could build a hospital, but later, I realized how specialized and complex hospital construction is. These delays drained my finances and tested my patience. It was a turning point—I needed guidance, or I risked losing everything.

How The Doctorpreneur Academy Changed the Game

While struggling with construction issues and financial stress, I came across The Doctorpreneur Academy—a community that supports doctors in setting up and scaling their own healthcare ventures.

It turned out to be the missing piece in my journey. The Academy provided step-by-step advice on hospital setup, from infrastructure planning to financial management. I learned to optimize costs and avoid costly mistakes. Whenever challenges arose, the Doctorpreneur Academy team was available to help me navigate them.

With expert mentorship, I successfully expanded from a 50-bed plan to a fully operational 100-bed hospital. I also learned how to make calculated decisions and avoid financial pitfalls.

I had only planned for 50 beds, but with the Doctorpreneur Academy's support, I gained the confidence to scale up. It was the best decision I made.

Lessons for Doctors Dreaming of Their Own Hospital

My experience serves as a valuable guide for doctors looking to start their own healthcare setup:

- Choosing the right architect and contractor is crucial. Working with professionals who specialize in hospital construction can save time and money.
- Every detail, from infrastructure to staffing, needs careful thought.

- Construction projects often take longer than expected, so having a backup plan is essential.
- Seeking expert guidance through platforms like The Doctorpreneur Academy can prevent costly mistakes.
- A well-planned hospital runs smoothly and avoids future operational issues.

City vs. Hometown: Where Should Doctors Set Up Practice?

I faced an important decision—should I establish my hospital in a big city or a smaller town? Big cities offer advanced facilities but come with intense competition. Small towns lack medical infrastructure but offer immense growth opportunities for doctors.

I chose to build my hospital in a rural area where access to healthcare was limited. It was a decision that changed lives—thousands of women and families now have access to quality medical care without having to travel long distances.

Inspiration for Future Doctorpreneurs

My journey proves that with the right guidance, resilience, and planning, doctors can transform their dreams into reality. For those looking to start their own hospitals, the path is tough, but success is achievable with expert mentorship and a strategic approach.

I now hope that my story will inspire others to take the leap and bring quality healthcare to places that need it the most.

Dr.Gangambika
Gynecologist
Talikoti, Karnataka

CHAPTER 12

A DOCTOR'S JOURNEY FROM 0 TO 1,00,000 SUBSCRIBERS ON YOUTUBE

Dr. G Buvaneswari,
MBBS, DGO, DNB - Obstetrics & Gynaecology.
Infertility Specialist, Laparoscopic Surgeon (Obs & Gyn),

A Humble Beginning.

I was born and raised in the quiet town of Rajapalayam, nestled in southern India. From a very young age, I dreamed of making a difference. As the first doctor from my community, I quickly learned that hard work would be the key to unlocking the doors of opportunity. Education became my guiding light, and with the unwavering support of my family, I nurtured an ambition to serve people through medicine.

It wasn't just academics that drove me—my natural empathy and desire to heal others laid the foundation for the path I chose.

The Journey of Training

My medical journey took me from Tiruppattur to Salem, and eventually to CMC Vellore—one of the most respected medical institutions in southern India. There, I pursued my postgraduate studies, immersing myself in the demanding world of infertility and obstetrics & gynaecology.

The intense hours, the exposure to complex cases, and the opportunity to learn from incredible mentors only deepened my resolve. My time in Chennai, too, was a turning point—it tested my limits, sharpened my knowledge, and prepared me for the road ahead.

A Pioneering Spirit

In 2011, driven by a dream to bring global expertise back to India, I took a bold step. I travelled to Cambridge to specialise in reproductive medicine and later to Germany for advanced endoscopy training. This was no small feat—I had two small children at the time, and financially, things weren't easy. But my determination pushed me forward.

Learning from some of the best minds at Cambridge was a transformative experience. It broadened my outlook, deepened my belief in evidence-based medicine, and completely changed how I approached infertility care.

The Impact of the Pandemic.

Then came the COVID-19 pandemic in 2020—a challenge none of us were prepared for. My practice in Chennai, like many others, faced immense uncertainty. Hospitals were overwhelmed, safety became a daily concern, and patient care had to adapt to a new normal.

I had to make difficult decisions, balancing my commitment to my patients while protecting my team. It was during this time that I truly understood the importance of innovation in medicine, not just clinically, but in how we reach and care for people.

The Doctorpreneur Academy

Looking for guidance in navigating this unfamiliar territory, I joined the Doctorpreneur Academy. It was a decision that changed the trajectory of my professional life. I moved from being solely a practitioner to embracing my role as an entrepreneur.

The Doctorpreneur academy has given confidence and boosted the morale about how to sustain in such a competitive world and corporate culture. Introduced the proper SOPs, manuals, and all documents for compliance to run a hospital. That made it impossible to possible.

The academy introduced me to digital platforms, sustainable business models, and innovative ways to extend my impact. It was here that I realised I could touch lives far beyond the walls of my clinic.

Becoming a YouTube Influencer.

In 2014, I took another leap, launching my YouTube channel. My goal was simple: educate and empower people with accurate, easy-to-understand medical information.

The response was overwhelming. Viewers connected with the honesty, clarity, and compassion in my videos. As I simplified complex concepts and addressed real concerns, my channel grew organically, soon crossing 100,000 subscribers. Through this platform, I became more than a doctor; I became a trusted voice for thousands seeking reliable healthcare guidance.

Ensuring Patient Care

Even as my digital presence grew, my focus on patient care never wavered. I implemented strict protocols to ensure every patient received the highest standard of treatment, even during the chaos of the pandemic.

Staying true to ethical, compassionate medicine is something I hold close to my heart. It's what defines my practice and the trust I've built over the years.

Setting Up an IVF Centre

One of my proudest accomplishments was setting up my own IVF centre. This was not just a professional milestone—it was a mission to bring hope to couples struggling with infertility.

From the emotional challenges to the technical intricacies, IVF is a journey that demands expertise and empathy. I made it my responsibility to walk that path with my patients, supporting, guiding, and celebrating every success along the way.

Practical Lessons in Cost-Cutting and Finances

As I grew into the role of a doctorpreneur, I realized the importance of financial sustainability. I learned how to optimize resources, reduce unnecessary costs, and still deliver exceptional care.

These lessons weren't just useful for me—they've become insights I now share with fellow doctors looking to build and grow their practices.

Delegation of Work and HR Challenges

Leading a healthcare team brought its own set of challenges. From hiring the right people to building a culture of shared values, I had to navigate the complexities of HR and leadership.

I developed systems for effective delegation, streamlined workflows, and focused on building a team that believed in our mission. And with my deep passion for teaching, I transformed our fertility centre into a training institute, ensuring that the next generation of reproductive health specialists continues to raise the bar.

A Message for My Fellow Doctors

To all my colleagues: Stay resilient. Embrace the changes around you, but never lose sight of why you started this journey—to heal, to serve, to make a difference.

Medicine is evolving, and so must we. With a strong sense of purpose and a positive mindset, we can overcome any challenge that comes our way.

Working Against All Odds

My story is one of perseverance. Whether it was travelling across continents with little savings, managing practice during a global crisis, or breaking digital barriers in healthcare, I've faced many challenges, but I never gave up.

Innovation, adaptability, and staying true to my values helped me rise above the odds.

My Legacy and Ongoing Journey

From a curious girl in Tirupattur district to a gynaecologist, IVF expert, and digital health educator—I've come a long way. But this is only the beginning.

My legacy lies not only in the patients I've treated but in the minds I've educated, the teams I've built, and the values I've shared. I hope my journey inspires others to dream beyond the conventional, to serve with compassion, and to never stop learning.

Dr. G Buvaneswari.

MBBS, DGO, DNB - Obstetrics & Gynaecology.
Infertility Specialist, Laparoscopic Surgeon (Obs & Gyn),

CHAPTER 13

THE GREEN DOCTOR: HEALING WITH NATURE, NOT JUST MEDICINE

Dr. Jaya Chandra Mohan
MBBS MD (ANAESTHESIA)
Natural healer

A Dream Rooted in Purpose

I didn't become a doctor because it was a safe career choice. My reason was deeply personal. When I was younger, I lost my grandmother, the person I loved the most. She was scared of hospitals and surgeries, but had no option when her condition worsened. She underwent surgery… and never came back. That moment changed me forever. I promised myself that I would become a doctor, not just to treat diseases, but to truly heal people. To give them hope. To make sure their families didn't go through the pain I did.

Building a Hospital Out of Thin Air.

Fifteen years ago, I had a dream of starting a hospital in Narayanpet. The estimated cost was around ₹2 crore. I had no investors, no backup, not even savings that came close. But I had something stronger: a vision and unshakable belief.

I practised manifestation every single day. I would close my eyes and see the hospital running, the patients recovering, the doctors working joyfully. Slowly, the universe responded. Brick by brick, my dream took shape.

Today, that dream is a 50-bedded multi-specialty hospital—the largest private healthcare setup in the district. My wife, a dedicated gynaecologist, works beside me. Together, we've made it our mission to serve the people of this region with compassion and integrity.

From Doctor to Nature Healer

Despite being an anaesthetist, I was never fully satisfied with only pills and procedures. Over time, my health began to reflect the stress, high cholesterol, and rising blood pressure. I didn't want to live on tablets, and I knew there had to be a better way.

That's when I turned to nature.

I began to explore many things from past wisdom:

- Fasting regularly
- Practising yoga and meditation
- Drinking alkaline water
- Growing my organic food.

I stopped all medications and embraced a completely plant-based lifestyle. The results were profound. My lab reports normalized, my energy returned, and something deep inside me shifted I felt alive.

I started making my own needs, which included toothpaste, shampoo, and even herbal drinks. I created a green lifestyle for myself, and then extended it to my patients. At my hospital, every visitor gets alkaline water and fermented health drinks daily in the morning, free of cost more than 5 years. Because I believe:

"Food is medicine. The kitchen is the real hospital." And made more than 20000 families follow this old tradition of making malt with Millets in their respective homes.

Healing Beyond Prescriptions

With time, I started applying natural healing practices to my patients, too. I've helped many people reverse chronic conditions like:

- Diabetes
- Obesity
- Infertility
- Hypertension
- Even some cancer cases

My protocol is simple, yet powerful:

- Clean, plant-based food
- Yogic breathing

- Detox through fasting
- Alkaline hydration
- Guided meditation and lifestyle shifts

This isn't an alternate system—it's ancient wisdom. And it works.

Scaling the Message with Doctorpreneur Academy

I always knew I wanted to reach more people. But I didn't know how. I had a website but no real social media presence. That's when I came across Doctorpreneur Academy.

The moment I joined, I felt like I had found my tribe—doctors who think differently, who want to create impact, not just income.

With their help, I:

- Started social media marketing
- Partnered with a professional agency
- Began planning webinars and online health education
- Learned how to delegate hospital work to focus on mission-based initiatives

I now dream of building digital ecosystems—courses, apps, content—that can bring this healing philosophy to every corner of India.

Family, Legacy & the Future

My elder son is studying MBBS, and my daughter is finishing school. I'm slowly bringing my son into this vision—not just to become a doctor, but to be a healer, an innovator, and a conscious entrepreneur.

What Doctorpreneur Academy Taught Me

Joining the academy gave me something I was missing—clarity. I learned:

- How to systematize my services
- The basics of digital branding and automation
- How to think long-term as a healthcare entrepreneur
- And most importantly, that I'm not alone on this journey

"I always wanted to serve people differently, but didn't know how. Doctorpreneur Academy gave me the structure and community I needed."

My Message to Fellow Doctors

To every young doctor, I want to say this:

Healing doesn't begin with a prescription pad. It begins with empathy, with food, with breath, with belief. We don't just need more doctors. We need healers. Builders. Visionaries. And above all, systems that work.

Invest in yourself. Learn digital tools. Build your ecosystem. And always remember—the power to transform lives lies in your hands.

From Narayanpet to the world, this is just the beginning.

Let's heal, grow, and serve—naturally.

By Dr. Jaya Chandra Mohan
MBBS MD (ANAESTHESIA)
Natural healer

CHAPTER 14

A GYNAECOLOGIST TEACHING MOMS ONLINE!

Dr. Jyoti MD DGO
Obstetrician and Gynaecologist
Thrissur, Kerala

From Hesitation to Purpose: My Journey as a Digital Gynaecologist

I never imagined I'd become a doctor, let alone a gynaecologist navigating both the delivery room and the digital world. I once dreamt of being a homemaker, content with a simple life. But life, as always, had other plans. Influenced by peers and circumstances, I accepted an MBBS seat.

I wasn't sure at the time, but somewhere deep down, I trusted that it was leading me to something meaningful.

Shifting Paths: How I Found My Passion in Gynaecology

After MBBS, I was inclined toward dermatology. But destiny had a twist in store. I got an opportunity to practice gynaecology, and something clicked. The connection with women, the impact I could make during pregnancy and delivery—it was profound. I didn't look back. That unexpected switch gave me a deeper purpose, one I didn't even know I was searching for.

The Pandemic Push: Losing My Channel, Finding My Voice

During the COVID-19 lockdown, I started experimenting with digital platforms to educate patients—YouTube Live sessions, webinars, anything that helped me stay connected. And just when I thought I was gaining momentum, I lost my entire YouTube channel. It was heartbreaking. But instead of giving up, I began again. I reorganized my patients into WhatsApp groups and started sending them pregnancy-related videos tailored to their journey. Those small digital communities became safe spaces for learning and support.

Juggling Clinic and Courses: My Dream Team

Balancing offline consultations with online education isn't always easy, but with the right support, it's absolutely possible. I'm fortunate to work alongside a dedicated physician assistant and a close friend, and together we make sure that every patient—whether in person or online—receives the care and attention they need. Platforms like Mind Valley played a pivotal role in helping me rediscover my passion and find a deeper purpose beyond the routine of a gynaecologist's daily practice. Over time, I began evolving—not just as a doctor, but also as a digital educator.

Championing HRT, Mind-Body Healing, and the Microbiome Revolution

I've become a passionate advocate for hormone replacement therapy (HRT), mind-body medicine, and microbiome health—areas that are often overlooked or misunderstood. I've seen firsthand how HRT can dramatically enhance the quality of life for menopausal women, and it's heartening to see research finally validating what many of us in clinical practice have long believed to be true.

My journey into the world of the microbiome began around 2014, when I first learned that our bodies are home to more microbial cells than human ones. The idea that these tiny organisms could influence everything from our immunity and metabolism to our mood and mental clarity fascinated me. Since then, I've been dedicated to helping my patients understand the vital role of gut health, sleep, stress, and nutrition as the core pillars of healing.

Equally transformative has been my growing interest in the mind-body connection. Books like *The Biology of Belief* by Dr. Bruce Lipton and *Mind to Matter* by Dawson Church opened my eyes to the powerful interplay between our thoughts, emotions, and physical health. These insights deeply resonated with me, reinforcing what I've witnessed in practice—that true healing happens when we treat the whole person, not just the symptoms.

Empowering Pregnant Women: One Video at a Time

One of my biggest missions is to prepare expecting mothers for what lies ahead. I've seen how a little awareness can prevent panic in labour rooms. Through live sessions, visuals, and simple language, I try to make complex topics understandable. When a woman feels prepared, she's stronger, calmer, and more in control—and that's everything.

Fighting Misinformation with Real Talk

We're living in a world full of misinformation—especially in health. That's why I believe it's high time doctors stepped up on social media. Not for likes or fame, but to offer real, reliable knowledge. I host monthly Q&A sessions where I answer genuine patient queries. No filters, no fluff—just facts and empathy.

Reading, Reflecting, and Sharing

I'm always learning—constantly reading and reflecting to better understand the root causes of the challenges my patients face. I've found immense value in learning from authors who are experts in their unique niches. Each one offers a new lens through which to view health and healing.

Books like *Mind to Matter* by Dawson Church and *The Obesity Code* by Dr. Jason Fung have helped me simplify complex concepts and make them relatable for my patients. *Estrogen Matters* has deepened my understanding of hormone therapy and its critical role in women's health.

Equally impactful have been books that explore the emotional and psychological dimensions of health. *The Myth of Normal* by Dr. Gabor Maté opened my eyes to how early life trauma shapes adult health, while *The Body Keeps the Score* by Dr. Bessel van der Kolk powerfully illustrates how our bodies store unprocessed emotions. Even parenting books like *Hold On to Your Kids* have taught me how strong emotional bonds influence lifelong resilience.

Sharing the wisdom from these varied sources has not only helped me explain health better—but it's also built deeper, more trusting relationships with my patients. They see me not just as a doctor, but as someone who walks beside them, integrating science and soul on their path to healing.

The Turning Point: Doctorpreneur Academy

Joining Doctorpreneur Academy was a game-changer. I finally found a space where I could be a learner again. The community helped me:

- Get clarity in my content strategy
- Rebuild confidence after my YouTube setback
- Build structured courses
- Understand branding and outreach
- Connect with fellow doctorpreneurs on the same journey

I stopped feeling like I was doing this alone. It gave me the tools—and more importantly, the belief—that I could grow in a way that was both authentic and impactful.

Where I Stand Today: Blending Heart and Tech

Today, I call myself a digital gynaecologist—not just because I use technology, but because I've learned how to *connect* through it. Whether it's an expecting mother in my clinic or someone watching my videos at midnight, I want her to feel heard, informed, and supported.

My journey hasn't been linear. There were doubts, detours, and digital disasters. But I turned every challenge into a classroom—and every lesson into content that can help someone else.

I didn't just embrace technology.

I turned it into a bridge between trust and transformation.

Dr.Jyoti

Obstetrician and Gynaecologist
Kerala

CHAPTER 15

REAL HEROES: HOW WE BROUGHT MODERN HEALTHCARE TO A VILLAGE—OUR JOURNEY OF HEART, GRIT & VISION

Dr Kailas Sanamadikar
MBBS D.Ortho

Dr Vaishali Sanamadikar
BAMS M D (Ayurveda)
Village Jath District Sangli
Maharashtra

I'm Dr. Vishali, and my husband, Dr. Kailash, this is the story of how two first-generation doctors built more than a hospital—we built a healthcare movement in our hometown of Jath.

Jath is a drought-prone town, tucked away from the spotlight, where even basic medical services were once a luxury. For the past 27 years, this is where we've lived, served, struggled, and grown—with nothing but a shared dream: to bring modern, ethical, and accessible healthcare to our people.

From Humble Beginnings to Purposeful Practice

Both of us come from families with no medical background. We were the first doctors in our families—and that made our vision deeply personal. After completing our respective trainings—Kailash in orthopaedics and me in Ayurveda—we returned to Jath, not because it was easy, but because it was necessary.

We started small. A modest clinic. Few patients. Limited resources. But what we had in abundance was commitment. Slowly, that clinic became the foundation of a hospital that now serves thousands.

Why We Decided to Build a Hospital in Jath

We've always believed that rural India deserves the same quality of care as metros. That belief turned into action when we decided to invest our savings—and hearts—into building a multi-specialty hospital right here in Jath.

It wasn't easy. Building credibility in a town where people were used to travelling 100+ kilometres for treatment took time. But with consistent effort, honesty, and a growing team, things began to shift.

Creating Infrastructure and Human Power

It wasn't just about machines or buildings. We quickly realised that rural India didn't just lack facilities—it lacked trained professionals.

So we started a nursing college to train local talent. Today, many of our own students work in hospitals across the region. We set up a blood bank, CT scan, and sonography unit—because no one should lose a loved one while waiting for a diagnosis.

When we introduced ICU services, it was a game-changer for emergency care. And recently, we achieved NABH accreditation—a proud moment for our entire team.

Fueling a Local Economy, Not Just Healing

Our commitment wasn't just clinical—it was community-wide. To support operations and generate jobs, we started a petrol pump and a transport company. These ventures helped us create employment and also supported the logistics of running a rural hospital.

We now treat around 1,200 OPD patients and 100 IPD patients every month—not just from Jath, but neighbouring towns as well.

Learning to Think Like Entrepreneurs

Honestly, for the longest time, we were just doctors doing our best. But something shifted when we joined Doctorpreneur Academy.

The academy gave us clarity on things we never learned in medical school:

- How to scale without burning out
- How to brand ourselves ethically and build visibility

- How to delegate smartly (we now outsource social media and digital marketing)
- How to set up systems for sustainable operations
- And most importantly, how to lead with vision and not just workload

We've even started exploring teleconsultations and advanced services like dialysis and MRI, which were once unimaginable in a town like ours.

What Keeps Us Going

It's the faces of people who no longer have to travel hours for a simple ultrasound.

It's the young nurses and technicians who say, "We got our first job because of you."

It's the families who bring us homemade sweets on discharge day, because their loved one was treated with dignity and care.

This is more than just a hospital—it's our life's work.

Our Vision Ahead

We're now working on expanding our hospital further—with more beds, more departments, and more teaching initiatives. We want to start structured academic programs, and even bring specialists from cities to work with us.

But more than anything, we want to prove that rural doesn't mean second-grade.

Final Thoughts

We're not superheroes. We're two doctors who believed that the best way to change the system was to start where it was broken. With the right mindset, community trust, and platforms like Doctorpreneur Academy, we've gone from local healers to healthcare entrepreneurs with a mission.

Our message to every doctor out there: You don't need a metro address to build world-class care. You just need heart, strategy, and the will to serve.

Dr Kailas Sanamadikar

MBBS D.Ortho

Dr Vaishali Sanamadikar

BAMS M D (Ayurveda)
Village Jath District Sangli
Maharashtra – Proudly Healing India's Heartland

CHAPTER 16

A JOURNEY OF RESILIENCE, REINVENTION, AND WELLNESS: MY STORY

Dr Kavita Jain
MBBS, DGO
Obstetrician and Gynaecologist
New Delhi

*I*f you had told the younger me—fresh out of medical college, brimming with dreams and determination—that life would test me in ways no textbook ever could, I might've smiled politely and shrugged it off. But today, as I sit in my clinic, *Wellness of Women*, I see my journey not just as a career, but as a story of trials and tribulations, starting, restarting, breaking & healing and rebuilding—again and again.

From Dreams in Delhi to Medical Reality

My story begins in the heart of Delhi. I completed Class 12 from Lady Irwin School, Connaught Place, and in 1989, I cleared the All India CBSE PMT. Due to administrative irregularities in the early days of that exam, I had to wait longer than expected for an allotment of my college. After a long, long wait for my seat, I got my allotment at Shri M.P. Shah Medical College in Jamnagar in Gujarat, in February 1990.

Five years later, armed with my MBBS degree, I returned to Delhi, did my internship and a house job in General Surgery at Hindu Rao Hospital. But it was women's health that truly called to me. So, back to Jamnagar I went, this time to pursue a Postgraduate diploma in Obstetrics and Gynaecology. I completed it in 1998, hopeful and ready.

Early Struggles and Silent Frustrations

But Delhi didn't open its arms to me as warmly as I'd hoped. Despite my qualifications, senior residency positions in government hospitals stayed out of reach—mostly because I didn't have the "right contacts." It was disheartening, but I didn't let that define me.

Instead, I took the less glamorous but equally important path—working in various private hospitals, gathering experience in my specialty as well as real-world experience of life and how the world and people are. Worked at different setups, gaining surgical hands-on experience and management of patients.

A Personal Battle Behind the White Coat

In 2002, I got married. I hoped that marriage would be a partnership built on trust, faith, care, love and understanding. My marital life was not as rosy as one imagines it to be. I kept on trying and make it work, coming from a conservative background, I had seen girls adjusting in families. But by 2010, it was painfully clear, after going through so much anguish, pain, that I was fighting a losing battle. After so much waste of time, opportunities, energy, efforts,and heart-shattering pain,I made the hardest decision of my life— I walked away.

With a heavy and broken heart but a firm resolve to heal myself to restart my life, I returned to Delhi and moved back in with my parents. That chapter of heartbreak also marked the beginning of my reinvention.

Rebuilding From Scratch

I started again—this time as a junior consultant in a private hospital in Gurgaon building,, learning again, treating patients and healing myself. The lines from my favourite poem DON'T QUIT …" when the funds are low, but the debts are high,and you want to smile but you have to sigh …" I kept on moving, kept on trying and regaining my lost confidence,and worked there for 5 years.Later, I moved to Delhi, I joined a reputed hospital in South Delhi as a consultant gynaecologist, where I am still working. With every patient I treated, every sleepless night on call, I was not just healing others—I was healing myself too.

Still, something tugged at me. A dream. A vision. A place of my own, where I could do more than just treat illness. I wanted to nurture wellness.

The Birth of Wellness for Women

All this while working at my hospital, I was also searching for the appropriate place to start my own clinic. As a gynaecologist, I needed a welcoming waiting area, a private consulting chamber and space for sterilization and autoclaving. These were non-negotiable.

And then, it happened.

With great support from my brother— who is a dermatologist who believed in me even when I doubted myself—I found it.

On February 7, 2021, I launched my clinic, named it, THE WOW CLINIC (*Wellness of Women*). A name born from personal pain and professional passion.

Because to me, a woman's health isn't just physical—it's emotional, mental, and spiritual. My mission was to build a space where women could feel seen, heard, and empowered.

Prevention Over Cure

Today, my work is not just about diagnosis and treatment. It's about education. When I see most of the gynaecological diseases like PCOS, infertility, abnormal uterine bleeding etc, I also see the root causes: stress, anxiety, poor diet and lifestyle choices, lack of physical movement, and emotional and mental neglect.

So I started guiding my patients on the correct lifestyle, clean and healthy eating, yoga & meditation, and self-care. I remind them that their wellness is the result of a correct mindset, taking care of their body, and correct goals in terms of especially profession and relationships. If your mind, body and work are prioritised in the right direction, you will be free from so many unnecessary problems of life.

More Than Medicine: My Life Beyond the Clinic

Outside the clinic, I'm a student of life. I practice yoga. I go for morning runs. I meditate. And music? That's my soul language. One day, I hope to take professional music lessons.

These rituals don't just help me cope—they keep me *alive*.

Words to the Young and Hopeful

If you're a young doctor reading this, here's what I want to tell you:

- Don't wait for perfect conditions—start small and start early, take strong decisions even if it means going against stereotypical social conditioning.
- Take control of your money, learn to manage your money yourself judiciously. Your bank account should be a single bank account, not a joint account with anyone who so whatsoever it may be.
- Don't lose your opportunities for anyone, no one will stand for you. Only you have to stand up for yourself. People give empty words of sympathy. But Pain, a very Deep pain which can't be put in words, is only for you to bear
- Develop your skills, keep learning, applying, learning more applications. Be a lifelong learner.
- Mindset matters more than medicine.

Doctorpreneur Academy: My Launchpad

In 2021, I joined Doctorpreneur Academy. That's when things really started falling into place. It gave me direction on branding, managing Google reviews, and creating a digital presence.

I went from being hesitant with technology to confidently building my clinic's online identity. The Academy gave me not just tools—it gave me *belief*.

By 2025, I plan to launch a full-fledged YouTube channel, along with an active Facebook and Instagram presence. It's already unfolding beautifully.

Living the Wellness I Preach

Wellness of Women is more than a clinic. It's a sanctuary.

And I'm more than a doctor—I'm a wellness warrior, a woman who rose from the ashes, and a guide for others navigating their own storms.

Life didn't go as planned—but I found my purpose anyway. And if my story can light the path for even one woman out there—patient or doctor—it's all worth it.

Because healing doesn't just happen on the exam table. Sometimes, it begins with a story.

And this was mine.

I would end with the poem of Robert Frost …

"Woods are lovely, dark and deep,

But I have promises to keep,

And miles to go before I sleep,

And miles to go before I sleep."

Dr Kavita Jain

MBBS, DGO
Obstetrician and Gynaecologist
New Delhi

CHAPTER 17

DR. KIRAN AMBEKAR'S AYURVEDIC WISDOM – HELPING PATIENTS NATURALLY

Dr. Kiran Ambekar
BAMS
Consulting Ayurvedic physician, Mumbai

I'm Dr. Kiran Ambekar, an Ayurvedic physician practising in Borivali East, Mumbai—and for the past four decades, I've had the privilege of walking hand-in-hand with my patients on their journey toward health, healing, and wholeness.

A Humble Beginning with a Spiritual Touch

My journey didn't begin with a big dream or a grand vision. Like many others, I once aspired to become an MBBS doctor, but fate had other plans. When I didn't secure an MBBS seat, I chose BAMS. At the time, it felt like a compromise. But over the years, I came to realise it was divine guidance. Ayurveda—with its rich roots in Sanskrit, classical sciences, and holistic healing—felt like home to me. Looking back, I have nothing but gratitude for the path I was put on.

Transitioning to Pure Ayurveda

In the initial years of my career, I practiced a mix of general and Ayurvedic medicine. It was a way to meet people where they were and gradually introduce them to the depth of Ayurvedic healing. But by 1994, I decided to walk fully on the path of Ayurveda. It was not just a professional decision—it was a personal commitment to purity, tradition, and trust in nature's wisdom.

Ayurveda, for me, is not just about herbs and oils. It's a system born from thousands of years of experience, intuition, and reverence for life. Every pulse I check, every lifestyle I analyse, I do so with this deep-rooted belief in the science.

Healing Through Experience: Clinical Cases That Inspire

Over the years, I've had the honor of treating many chronic and lifestyle-related conditions. One case that stands out was a diabetic patient with an HbA1c of 9. With the right Ayurvedic diet, medication, and lifestyle changes, we brought it down to 7 within a month. No insulin. No side effects. Just discipline and nature working hand in hand.

My focus has always been on conservative, effective care, minimising hospital visits and avoiding unnecessary interventions wherever possible.

I believe that if we listen closely enough, the body always tells us what it needs.

The Backbone of My Journey: My Family

None of this would've been possible without the unwavering support of my family. My mother, now 90, remains my greatest inspiration—her strength still guides me every day. My wife, Anjali, a librarian with Bharatiya Vidyabhawan, has been my constant companion in this journey. She helps me organise knowledge sessions and encourages my ongoing learning. I consider her my silent co-healer.

Embracing the Digital Age

Even after 40+ years in practice, I believe learning never stops. That's why I recently started organising webinars and workshops—one of which was on varicose veins, and it received a great response. Now, I'm preparing a session on managing **Diabetes and Obesity** through Ayurveda.

These public engagements give me energy. They keep me young at heart and connected with people.

The Doctorpreneur Academy – A Turning Point

Joining the **Doctorpreneur Academy** as a **Diamond Member** has been nothing short of transformational. It gave me the tools, mindset, and community I didn't even know I was missing. From weekly mentoring to digital literacy and branding guidance—it has opened doors I once thought were locked.

Now, I'm working on launching structured digital programs and stepping into the world of **social media**, one platform at a time. I often say, *"I don't know exactly how I'll evolve—but I do know this is the right path."* And that belief alone keeps me moving.

A Message to Fellow Practitioners

To every young doctor, every Ayurvedic practitioner out there—I want to say this: *"Age is no barrier to service. If your intention is right, the universe will support you."*

Let us keep learning, keep serving, and never stop believing in the power of natural healing. If I can take my practice digital in my 60s, so can you.

Dr. Kiran Ambekar
BAMS
Consulting Ayurvedic physician, Mumbai

CHAPTER 18

FROM SMALL TOWN DOCTOR TO YOUTUBE STAR: MY JOURNEY DR KISHAN BHAGWAT

Dr. Kishan R. Bhagwat
MBBS, MS (Ortho – PGI Chandigarh),
DNB (Ortho), MCh (Ortho), DipSICOT (Belgium)
CEO & Senior Consultant Orthopaedic and Joint Replacement Surgeon,
Bhagwat Hospital, Sagar

I still remember the narrow lanes of Sagar in Karnataka—the peaceful town where my journey began. A place steeped in tradition, devotion, and the quiet rhythm of community life. Born into a family of doctors—my father, a gynaecologist, and my mother, a general practitioner—our home often felt like a small hospital. Watching them serve with compassion sparked a calling in me from a very young age.

Following the White-Coated Footsteps

It felt only natural to walk the same path. I studied hard, topped the Karnataka CET, and earned a seat at Mysore Medical College. Later, I cleared the PGI Chandigarh entrance on my first attempt and chose orthopaedics—a decision that shaped my future.

During my MS at PGI, I discovered a deep passion for academics and research, publishing 13 papers in indexed international journals. Many assumed I would stay in academia. But my heart? It was already yearning for home.

Coming Home with a Purpose

After completing my postgraduation, I joined a 200-bed hospital in Shimoga, where I introduced joint replacement surgeries and handled complex trauma cases. But every weekend, I found myself back in Sagar, conducting outreach OPDs. What began as routine soon became a calling.

Eventually, I returned full-time to our family's modest 30-bed hospital. Taking over the reins, I led its transformation—first to 50 beds, then a 100-bed multispecialty facility with three modular OTs, advanced diagnostics, and a committed consultant team. Today, with 11 full-time consultants, we serve patients from across Karnataka.

The Real Challenge – Building a Team

The toughest challenge wasn't infrastructure—it was people. Attracting and retaining skilled talent in a Tier-3 town is no small task. Instead of chasing big resumes, we focused on culture. We introduced role-playing-based training, celebrated small staff victories, and fostered a workplace where everyone felt valued. That sense of purpose became our secret ingredient.

Spiritual Roots and Social Responsibility

My professional life is deeply intertwined with my spiritual journey. As a certified Vedic instructor and an active member of the Sri Sathya Sai Seva Organisation, I teach Vedic chants weekly and regularly participate in free medical camps.

Along with my family, we've adopted three villages where we provide routine health checkups, moral education in schools, and other welfare programs. For me, medicine has never been just about healing bodies—it's about nurturing souls.

Going Digital – My YouTube Leap.

March 2023 marked a new chapter. I uploaded my first YouTube video—simple orthopaedic tips in Kannada. I didn't expect much, just hoped someone might benefit.

But the response surprised me. Views grew, and so did heartfelt comments. Today, my channel has over 2.6 lakh subscribers. I share two videos every week, answering real patient questions in a language they understand. Patients now travel over 500 km to consult me, often saying, "Doctor, we already feel like we know you."

That's the power of digital connection—and it has transformed how I serve.

Marketing with Meaning

To celebrate 40 years of our hospital, we didn't throw a party. Instead, we launched eight weeks of community service—walkathons, geriatric camps, women's health drives, and a sanitation worker appreciation day. These events not only deepened our connection with the community but also, brought in new patients who resonated with our values.

Joining Doctorpreneur Academy – A Game Changer

My biggest mindset shift came after joining the Doctorpreneur Academy. At first, I was skeptical—what could an orthopaedic surgeon from Sagar really gain from an online academy? But the One Day One Video challenge gave me on-camera confidence. The Quantum Membership taught me things med school never did—HR practices, leadership strategies, procurement planning, and digital branding.

It helped me marry clinical expertise with entrepreneurial thinking. That blend transformed both our hospital and outreach.

Final Thoughts

From the narrow streets of Sagar to digital screens across Karnataka, my journey proves that impact doesn't require a metro address or massive capital. What it does require is clear intent, a service mindset, and the courage to evolve. To every young doctor reading this—especially those from small towns—remember: your story matters. And the world is waiting to hear it.

Dr. Kishan R. Bhagwat

MBBS, MS (Ortho – PGI Chandigarh),
DNB (Ortho), MCh (Ortho), DipSICOT (Belgium)

CHAPTER 19

INCREDIBLE JOURNEY OF FRCS TO FOUNDER: MY JOURNEY BACK HOME

Dr. Manjunath
MS, FRCS Orthopaedics
Tumkur, Karnataka

*M*y story isn't just about a doctor returning home—it's about resilience, reinvention, and redefining patient care in India. I'm Dr. Manjunath, an orthopaedic surgeon with an FRCS degree, trained and seasoned in the UK. For years, I thrived in an environment of surgical excellence, mastering everything from knee arthroscopy to complex shoulder procedures. But despite the success, something inside me kept pulling me back, to my roots, to India.

The UK Chapter: Growth Through Discomfort

When I first left for the UK, I wasn't chasing a dream. It was more of a practical decision, driven by ambition, opportunity, and financial constraints. Honestly, I was reluctant. But once there, I immersed myself fully, learning cutting-edge techniques and understanding that medicine is not static—it evolves, and so must we.

I had everything a professional could ask for. Yet, something vital was missing—connection, purpose, and proximity to the people who mattered most.

Answering the Call: Why I Came Back

The decision to return to India was not a sudden one. My ageing parents needed me. I had watched friends struggle to care for their families from a distance, and I didn't want to make that same mistake. Beyond personal reasons, I began to feel a strong sense of duty—a calling to serve my community, to bring world-class orthopaedic care to Bangalore, and to do it on my own terms.

The Tough Start: Rebuilding from Zero

Coming back was not glamorous. I was no longer a well-known surgeon in a big system. I was just another name in a saturated, skeptical market. Patients didn't know me. Colleagues wondered why I left the UK. That phase was rough.

That's when I discovered the Doctorpreneur Academy. Their mentorship, resources, and mindset training opened my eyes. I wasn't just a doctor anymore—I was a founder. I learned to think like an entrepreneur without compromising my ethics or clinical standards.

Redefining Care: Communication Over Procedures

One of the biggest takeaways from the Academy was this: Skill is important, but trust is everything. Patients weren't just looking for a good surgeon—they were looking for someone who'd listen, explain, and care.

I made it a point to simplify medical jargon, to give my patients time, and to build genuine relationships. As a result, referrals began pouring in—not just for my surgical expertise but because people finally felt heard. And that changed everything.

Why I Chose Private Practice

I had stints in corporate hospitals, but the red tape, delayed decisions, and impersonal systems frustrated me. I didn't want to be a cog in a machine. I wanted freedom—to treat patients on my terms, to innovate, and to create something meaningful.

Private practice offered just that. With the Academy's guidance, I was able to confidently make that leap.

Smart Start: Rental Over Real Estate

I didn't want to be burdened by heavy EMIs or real estate investments right away. I started my clinic in a rented space—smart, flexible, and sustainable. It allowed me to channel my energy into delivering care, not worrying about overheads.

Going Digital: A Necessity, Not an Option

In today's world, being online is non-negotiable. The Doctorpreneur Academy helped me understand how to use tools like Google My Business,

Facebook, and online medical platforms effectively. I launched a simple, informative website, shared helpful content, and started engaging with patients online.

And it worked—people began to trust me even before walking into my clinic.

From One Doctor to Many

Today, I'm proud to say that my journey has inspired others, especially doctors who are abroad and wondering if returning home is worth it. My answer? Absolutely. With the right mindset, guidance, and systems, we can do more than just practice medicine—we can create impact.

The surgeries I perform are only one part of the story. The real success lies in the smiles, the trust, and the long-term relationships I've built.

A Message to My Fellow Doctorpreneurs

If you're a doctor dreaming of independence, of doing things differently, don't wait for the perfect moment. There's no "right time"—just a right intention backed by action.

The Doctorpreneur Academy gave me that framework, and I'm living proof that it works.

Coming home wasn't just the best decision for my family and me, it was the best decision for the countless lives I now touch every single day.

Dr. Manjunath
MS, FRCS Orthopaedics
Tumkur,
Karnataka

CHAPTER 20

ON A MISSION FOR A DEAFNESS FREE INDIA BY 2047

Dr. Manoj Kumar Gupta.
MBBS, MS(ENT)
ENT Surgeon, Educator, Author, and Mission-builder.
Varanasi, UP

$\mathcal{M}$ost people see hearing loss as a problem that only affects the elderly, or something that can wait. But I've seen how this "invisible disability" quietly robs people of connection, confidence, and opportunity. I'm Dr. Manoj Kumar Gupta, and I've made it my life's mission to change that.

As an ENT surgeon, educator, author, and founder of Eastern Uttar Pradesh's first ENT-focused hospital, I've stepped beyond the role of a doctor to become a voice for millions suffering in silence. My journey—from a secure government job to building a movement for a Deafness-free India by 2047— has been a relentless journey of purpose.

From Government Job to Purpose-Driven Path

I completed my MS in ENT in 2004. Like many of my peers, I took the traditional route, joining a government setup. But the longer I stayed, the more I felt like I was surviving, not serving. The urge to do something meaningful for the patients suffering from hearing loss, pushed me out of my comfort zone. Leaving a secure job wasn't easy, but it was necessary.

There were doubts. I questioned my surgical skills. I worried about patient flow. But that leap of faith turned into the foundation of my journey.

The AIIMS Experience and Global Learning

My time at AIIMS as a Senior Research Fellow under the able guidance of Prof.RC.Deka shaped me deeply. The exposure, the complexity, the discipline—it refined my clinical acumen. I also had the opportunity to work on WHO projects related to deafness, which broadened my view from individual care to community and global health. I started seeing hearing loss not just as a medical issue,but as a societal epidemic waiting to be addressed.

Building Satkriti Hospital: My Home Became My Mission Ground

In 2012, I laid the foundation for Satkriti Hospital in Varanasi. We didn't have a fancy setup. My own home became our first clinic. We turned the front area into a reception, bought a generator to tackle power cuts, and focused on one thing—impact.

Every brick laid was backed by belief, not budgets. My wife and I had left high-paying jobs to serve our people back home. It wasn't an easy call, but it was the right one.

Shifting Mindsets: From Fear of Loans to Financial Leverage

Earlier, the word "loan" made me uncomfortable. But I realised that if I wanted to grow and serve more people, I needed to invest—with courage and calculation. Whether it was medical equipment, staff training, or even my kids' education—I began leveraging finance wisely. EMIs, SIPs, strategic borrowing—these became tools, not traps.

Redefining Patient Care Through Ethics and Simplicity

To me, patient care isn't a transaction. It's a relationship. I don't believe in middlemen, manipulation, or marketing gimmicks. I believe in clarity, directness, and genuine service. We educate our patients, explain options, and give them the space to decide—without fear.

And yes, even small things matter—like a cool waiting area on a hot summer day, or a kind receptionist who makes someone feel heard.

The Power of Digital Presence: Branding Through Value

I started sharing small, simple videos on Instagram and YouTube—talking about hearing loss, its signs, and its solutions. People resonated. Not because the videos were flashy—but because they were honest. Today, patients come to us after watching a reel or reading a post. That's the power of personal branding in medicine. It's not about going viral. It's about building trust and awareness.

My Positive QR System and AI Tools for Feedback

Online reviews are tricky. I didn't want one angry voice to overpower a hundred grateful ones. So, we created a "Positive QR System" that encourages patients to share their experiences authentically. With the help of AI, we even assist them in writing meaningful reviews. It's innovative, it's fair—and it works.

Becoming an Author with a Message

My book, *Silent Epidemic: Unveiling the burden of Deafness in India*, was my way of turning knowledge into a movement. With blurbs by legends like Nasiruddin Shah and Amitabh Bachchan, the book addresses not just the problem—but what each of us can do about it. Awareness is the first surgery.

Delegation, Teamwork, and Time Management

As my mission scaled, I had to unlearn doing everything myself. I now work with a team—dedicated people who help manage operations, documentation, and outreach. With structured SOPs and defined roles, I finally found time to do what matters most—teach, operate, and advocate.

Satkriti: The First ENT-Focused Hospital in Eastern UP

We became the first ENT hospital in Eastern Uttar Pradesh with a NABH accreditation and a cooperative surgical model. We've received WHO grants and are working on joint ventures to add ENT wings in multispecialty hospitals across India—because access shouldn't be limited by geography.

Spreading Awareness, One Sunday at a Time

Every Sunday, we conduct free workshops. We distribute books, hold awareness drives, and educate schoolchildren, teachers, and rural communities. This isn't just outreach—it's prevention.

Satkriti Foundation

At Satkriti Foundation, we believe in the profound power of compassion, service, and healing. Guided by the principles of integrity, empathy, and a deep sense of purpose, our mission goes beyond just providing healthcare — it is a divine calling to uplift and transform lives.

In collaboration with Satkriti Hospital, we have provided free surgeries to over 700 patients under the Ayushman Bharat Scheme, and facilitated Cochlear Implant Surgeries for eligible patients under the State CI Fund Programme and ADIP-CI Programme.

The Doctorpreneur Academy Shift

Everything changed when I joined Doctorpreneur Academy.

It wasn't just about learning business—it was about transforming vision into action. I learned how to:

- Build scalable systems
- Communicate my message effectively
- Use branding ethically
- Lead a team with purpose
- Leverage finance without fear

The academy didn't just give me skills. It gave me direction, belief, and a community of fellow dreamers.

My Vision: Deafness Free India by 2047

This is more than a tagline. It's my life's mission.

Every patient we treat, every school we educate, every parent we empower—it all adds up. I'm building a national movement—one that removes stigma, promotes early detection, and makes ear care accessible to all.

I believe we can—and must—eradicate preventable hearing loss from India by 2047

Dr. Manoj Kumar Gupta

ENT Surgeon, Educator, Author, and Mission-builder.
Varanasi, UP

CHAPTER 21

DOCTOR TO ENTREPRENEUR: HOW I DID IT!

Dr. Manoj Kumar
MBBS, MS Gen. Surgery
Hissar, Haryana

From Surgeon to Doctorpreneur: My Journey with Navjeevan Multi- Speciality Hospital

In the heart of Hisar, Haryana, stands Navjeevan Multi-Speciality Hospital—a symbol of my journey from a government-employed surgeon to a full-time healthcare entrepreneur. It's more than just a hospital to me; it reflects years of grit, growth, and an unshakable belief that doctors can be more than just clinicians—we can be changemakers.

The Spark of Transformation

When I started my medical journey, I never imagined myself running a hospital. With an MBBS and an MS in General Surgery, I was posted in government hospitals near the India-Pakistan border at Gharsana and Anupgarg, located in Sri Ganganagar, Rajasthan, serving people in some of the most underserved and remote areas of our country. The work was noble and fulfilling—but over time, I began to feel a deeper calling.

I have two fellowships, Fellowship of the Indian Association of Gastrointestinal Endosurgeons FIAGES and Fellow of the Academy of Medical Sciences (FAMS) , and I wanted to do more. To create something of my own. That's when I stumbled upon mentorship programs like the Doctorpreneur Academy, which challenged my perspective and introduced me to the idea that doctors can also be business leaders. That seed of thought grew stronger with each passing day.

Taking the Leap

In 2014, I decided to take the plunge and start Navjeevan Multi-Speciality Hospital. It wasn't easy—far from it. Setting up a hospital meant facing bureaucratic hurdles, arranging finances, and constantly reassuring myself that I wasn't biting off more than I could chew.

One memorable moment still sticks with me—I appeared for a degree exam without formal preparation, on the encouragement of a junior. To my surprise, I cleared it. That small win rekindled a sense of belief in my capabilities, both academic and professional.

Discipline: The Bedrock of My Journey

My journey has always been driven by discipline. I do regular yoga, Pranayam and meditation. Back in 1990, when I cracked my entrance exam, it wasn't brilliance but consistency and time management that made it happen. Even during lunch breaks, I'd revise chapters. That habit of using every available moment has helped me immensely as an entrepreneur, where time is your most valuable currency and, I am thankful for my entire successful journey to God, my parents, family, teachers, and friends.

Early Career Lessons

Starting, even with a postgraduate qualification, the pay was modest, and the expectations were sky-high. It was frustrating. That imbalance—of giving more than receiving—was a wake-up call. It made me realise that if I wanted a system that rewarded hard work and encouraged growth, I'd have to build it myself.

Building Partnerships the Right Way

Over the years, I've learned a lot about partnerships. They're not just about sharing work—they're about mutual respect, communication, and clarity. I always say: put everything in writing. Roles, responsibilities,and terms—clarity prevents confusion. Whether short-term or long-term, successful partnerships need structure.

My Team, My Strength

I've never believed in running a one-man show. My team is my backbone. We keep communication open and meet regularly to align our goals. I make it a point to be present, to show up—not just physically, but with intent. Growth, for me, is something we build together.

Learning Never Stops

One of the biggest lessons I've learned is: never stop learning. I attend webinars, workshops, and anything that adds to my toolkit. I approach business growth the way I'd approach buying jewelry—you start with silver before jumping to gold or diamonds. That mindset of gradual, calculated growth has served me well, especially in adopting new services and tech.

To Young Doctors: Don't Forget Yourself

If there's one message I want to pass on to younger doctors, it's this: take care of your health and value your family. Don't burn out chasing early success. I've seen it too often—doctors giving their all to the system, only to end up exhausted and disconnected from their loved ones. Draw boundaries. Be present. That's real success.

Winning Trust, Patient by Patient

Not all patients understand or trust long-term care plans right away. But over time, as they begin to see results—more energy, better outcomes—the trust builds. That's when you realise that doing the right thing pays off, even if it takes time.

Doctorpreneur Academy: My Catalyst

Joining Doctorpreneur Academy was a turning point. It didn't just teach me about finance, marketing, and operations—it gave me a community of like-minded doctors. Through mentorship calls, strategy sessions, and structured content, I began to see my hospital not just as a clinic, but as a business with purpose. That clarity changed everything.

Looking Back and Moving Forward

From a surgeon serving in rural India to directing a multi-speciality hospital, my path hasn't been conventional. But it's mine—and it's deeply fulfilling. I've learned that limitations are just invitations to innovate. That with the right mindset, support, and systems, doctors can build something truly transformative.

Today, I proudly call myself a Doctorpreneur—a healer, a leader, and a student of life and business.

Dr. Manoj Kumar
MBBS, MS GEN SURGERY
Hissar, Haryana

CHAPTER 22

A DREAM ROOTED IN MY HOMETOWN TO SERVE THE MOTHERLAND

Dr. Muralidhara, MBBS, MS, DNB
Orthopaedic surgeon
Tumkur, Karnataka.

I'm Dr. Muralidhara, an orthopedic surgeon from Tumkur, Karnataka. I had all the accolades—gold medals, top ranks, and multiple degrees in orthopaedic surgery (MBBS, MS, DNB). Like many of my peers, I had the option to settle in a metro, earn well, and enjoy the perks of a high-flying urban lifestyle. But deep inside, I knew that wasn't my path.

Tumkur was calling me back. Not out of nostalgia—but responsibility. My parents were here, and so were countless people with limited access to quality orthopaedic care. I couldn't ignore the gap. So, I chose to return. Not because it was easy, but because it felt right.

Building from Scratch, with Purpose

Coming back home wasn't about opening a fancy clinic. It was about addressing a very real need. The infrastructure for advanced orthoapedic procedures here was barely functional. At times, I had to travel to Bangalore to borrow surgical instruments or implants. Imagine that—preparing for a major surgery and not even having the basic tools at hand.

But I refused to be discouraged. These challenges didn't break me—they shaped me. Every obstacle was a lesson. Every patient was a reason to keep going.

I Didn't Inherit a Hospital—So I Built One

Many doctors walk into well-established family practices or inherited hospitals. I didn't have that. I had to build from the ground up—brick by brick, decision by decision. That meant stepping out of my comfort zone and learning things no textbook ever taught me—planning infrastructure, managing people, handling finances, and embracing digital tools.

And in that process, something clicked. I realised I wasn't just a surgeon anymore—I was becoming a creator of systems, a builder of hope.

Morning Rituals That Kept Me Going

Running a hospital, performing surgeries, handling staff—it can wear you down. That's when I discovered the Morning Grace Rituals from the Doctorpreneur Academy. Meditation, affirmations, and visualization—simple yet powerful tools that kept me centred.

Every morning, I'd take time for myself before I gave myself to the world. Those few minutes helped me approach the day with clarity, energy, and purpose.

My Mission Took Me Online

Treating patients inside my hospital was one thing—but I wanted to reach beyond the walls. That's how I started making videos. Over time, I created more than 350 YouTube videos in Kannada, English, and other languages to spread awareness about bone and joint health.

From farmers in remote villages to youngsters dealing with sports injuries—people started finding answers through my videos. That became my second practice—an online OPD that never closed.

Thanks to the Doctorpreneur Academy, I learned how to use video-making not just for visibility, but for impact. I realised many patients don't even know what to ask—so I began answering unasked questions.

My Patients Gave Me More Than Money

Not everyone who comes to my hospital can afford expensive treatments. But they bring something more meaningful—blessings. Some offer coconuts, some bring homegrown fruits, others just hold my hand with tears in their eyes.

That's when I know—I made the right choice.

The Unasked Question

People often wonder—why would someone with my credentials choose a smaller town over a metro?

The truth is, I never needed luxury. I needed meaning.

I chose this path because:

- I wanted to give back to the land that raised me.
- I wanted to make healthcare more accessible.
- I truly believe one doctor, one hospital, one heart can make a difference.

My Legacy? A Life of Service

Today, my journey continues—not as a solo warrior, but as part of a growing community of doctorpreneurs, changemakers, and visionaries. I don't just want to be remembered as a surgeon. I want to be remembered as someone who *chose service over status, roots over riches, and legacy over luxury.*

And I hope my story reminds other doctors—you don't have to wait for a perfect system to create impact. Sometimes, all you need is *courage, commitment,* and a *deep love for your people.*

Dr.Muralidhara, MBBS, MS, DNB

Orthopedic surgeon
Tumkur Karnataka.

CHAPTER 23

FROM THE FIRST UROLOGIST IN KOLHAPUR TO A HEALTHCARE VISIONARY

Dr. Narendra Basarge
Urologist
MBBS & MS (General Surgery) from Baroda Medical College
M Ch (Urology) from SGPGIMS, Lucknow.
M Phill (Hosp & Health care Mgmt) from BITS, Pilani
FMAS.
Kolhapur, Maharashtra

- Director & Head, Basarge Urology Hospital and Lithotripsy Centre, Kolhapur.
- CEO and Chairman department of Urology, Vital Super speciality Hospital, Kolhapur.
- MCI recognised M Ch (urology) Guide and PG teacher.
- Ex.Asso Prof of Urology at KIMS (Krishna Institute of Medical Sciences), Karad.
- Visiting Consultant Urologist, DY Patil Medical College and Hospital, Kolhapur.

Introduction

I am Dr Narendra Basarge, a senior consultant urologist with over three decades of experience in the fields of General and endourology, andrology, reconstructive urology and kidney transplant surgery.

I was not born into a medical family — far from it, a middle-class family with a father serving in the central government and a mother serving as a primary school teacher. The importance of education and hard work was imbibed in my upbringing. But what I lacked in the family background of doctor parents, I could make up for with curiosity, consistency, and a strong belief that I could create meaningful change in healthcare. Today, looking back at my journey from a small clinic in Kolhapur to running a multispeciality hospital, mentoring young doctors, and embracing digital transformation, I can say with gratitude — it has indeed been a very fulfilling ride.

Humble Beginnings: The First Doctor in the Family

I was always drawn to biology. In school, I remember being fascinated by how the human body worked. I cleared my 12th standard with a high ranking in the board and was getting admission in all regional engineering colleges, including IIT, but had to wait a full year to get into medical school due to age restrictions. I was underage by one year and had not completed 17 years. Rather than wasting time, I self-studied anatomy. That one year gave me such a solid foundation that when I finally joined Baroda Medical College for MBBS and later MS, I stood out.

Training, Mentorship, and Inspiration

During my MS, I found myself gravitating toward urology. Urology is a speciality that requires precision, innovation, and is highly result-oriented ,giving rapid relief and cure to the patient. I was especially captivated by the evolving field of endoscopic urological surgery and kidney transplantation. My training across different apex institutions helped me to build a strong surgical foundation — but more than that, it gave me exposure to systems and mentors that raised my standards.

Choosing Kolhapur: Choosing Kolhapur, a type II city and a district place over metro cities, was a bold move after super-specialisation. I had multiple job offers from the metro cities and fellowship offers from abroad. Definitely, they could have provided much better infrastructure and paid salaries. However, I opted to return to Kolhapur — my hometown — where there was not a single M.Ch. Urologist at that time,and the practise of urology was in a rudimentary stage. It was definitely a very difficult decision to take, but now, retrospectively I feel it was a meaningful one. I started a small five-bedded setup near the railway station and began travelling to nearby districts for surgeries.

Building Trust Brick by Brick

Those early days were challenging. Every single patient mattered. I would carry my instruments, sometimes drive 30–40 km even for minor procedures — just to build trust. Those were the days when it was very difficult to get finances and loans from the bank. I remember, I wanted to purchase advanced endoscopes, and one of my patients signed the guarantee papers of the bank. Slowly, word spread. Patients started visiting from neighbouring districts and even Goa and North Karnataka. What I lacked in resources, I made up with relentless service.

No Leaves, Only Dedication

For the first five years, I didn't take a single day off. Sundays were reserved for district visits. I knew that in the long run, consistent effort would pay off. And it did. Not just in numbers, but in the depth of relationships I formed with patients and colleagues.

The Power of Communication and Decision-Making

Words of wisdom learned over the experience of so many years — surgery isn't just about skill. It's about wisdom. Knowing *when not to operate* is just as important. In my experience, 10% of success lies in technical skill; 90% is how you communicate, empathise, and make people feel safe and understood.

Physical Fitness, Golf, and Work-Life Balance

At 61, I'm still fit, active, and disease-free — something I credit to my passion for golf. I play daily for one and a half to two hours. It helps with developing hand-eye coordination, achieving flexibility of the body and a focused mind, and the same is required for performing a technically perfect surgery. It also gives me a mental break. I am now writing a book called *"Golfing the Surgeon's Way,* "where I draw parallels between surgical precision and the art of golfing.

Legacy Building: Teaching the Next Generation

My children have settled in the US, but my roots are firmly here. I have made it my mission to teach and mentor the next generation of doctors.

We have set up training programs in medical colleges, and my hospital now has 30 beds, modular operation theatres, state-of-the-art equipment, and we are in the process of starting a kidney transplant program in my hospital.

Never Stop Learning: A Course in Hospital Management

Even after 25+ years in practice, I felt the urge to learn more. I joined a healthcare management course from BITS Pilani and the University of Pennsylvania. Learning alongside hospital CEOs and senior professionals opened my eyes to leadership, systems thinking, and sustainable growth.

Advice for Young Doctors

To the young doctors reading this — don't rush into private practice. Give yourself at least five years after specialisation to build experience. Focus on upgrading your skills, especially in laparoscopy and newer technologies. And never stop learning — not just medicine, but communication, business, and ethics too.

Challenges in Urology and Why It's Worth It

Urology is capital-intensive. The machines, the infrastructure — it takes a toll. But it's worth it. The results are immediate and deeply satisfying. Removing a kidney stone and seeing the instant relief on a patient's face — there's no better feeling. Plus, it offers more stability and fewer emergencies.

Embracing Digital Transformation with Doctorpreneur Academy

Even as an established super specialist, I realised I wasn't leveraging the digital world. Joining Doctorpreneur Academy was a game-changer. I learned about online branding, Google reviews, patient communication, and the importance of visibility. Today, I'm not just running a hospital — I'm building a digital brand and planning for the future.

We're even exploring models to make the hospital public someday — making healthcare accessible, transparent, and sustainable.

Conclusion: A Legacy of Healing and Innovation

I didn't set out to be a visionary — I just wanted to serve. But over the years, that commitment has grown into something bigger than me. From setting up the first urology practice in Kolhapur to mentoring students and writing books, my mission now is to leave behind a healthcare ecosystem that outlives me.

Dr. Narendra Basarge

Urologist
MBBS & MS (General Surgery) M Ch (Urology).
M Phil (Hosp & Health care Mgmt) from BITS, Pilani, FMAS.
Kolhapur, Maharashtra

CHAPTER 24

REAL SOLUTIONS FOR FIXING HOSPITALS & TRAINING DOCTORS

Dr. Neeraj Bedi
MD PSM
Hospital Administrator

I didn't always dream of being a doctor. It was my mother's dream first. I still remember the look in her eyes whenever she spoke about it—with hope, pride, and unshakable belief. That dream became mine, and despite the pressure and uncertainty of PMT exams, I threw myself into the challenge with everything I had. I wasn't the brightest student in the room, but I was determined. And when I got my medical college admission, I knew I was stepping into something much bigger than just a career. It was the beginning of a life of purpose.

The Soul of Healthcare: Community Medicine

From the very beginning, I found myself drawn to the essence of medicine—the people, the stories, the everyday lives we often overlook. That's how I discovered the power of community medicine. While others raced toward super-specialisations, I chose to dive deep into what I believe is the backbone of healthcare—preventive, accessible, and people-centred care.

For me, community medicine is not a "supportive" subject—it's clinical, critical, and completely underrated. Family medicine, primary care, and preventive strategies are not just buzzwords. They are the anchors of any sustainable healthcare system, especially when we're dealing with chronic diseases, geriatric care, and underserved rural populations.

A Career that Merged Service and Systems

Over time, my path expanded beyond consultations and wards. I found myself leading hospitals—fixing what was broken, fighting red tape, and reviving institutions that had almost given up. I've faced just about every challenge one can in hospital administration: political interference, underpaid staff, crumbling infrastructure, and deep-rooted apathy. But I didn't walk away. I couldn't.

Instead, I rolled up my sleeves and started rebuilding from scratch. We got ventilators installed. Oxygen pipelines were connected. Outdated systems have been replaced. Suddenly, hospitals that barely functioned were saving lives—and doing it with dignity.

Putting Patients First in Public Healthcare

In my years working within government systems, one belief has guided every decision: people come first—always. Budget cuts and cost-saving shortcuts can never justify poor patient care. I've pushed hard for investments in infrastructure, medical equipment, and most importantly, in human resource development. Because the most advanced machine is useless without a well-trained, motivated team behind it.

I've also embraced technology—from digitising hospital processes to exploring AI in diagnostics. I truly believe the future of public healthcare lies in merging innovation with empathy.

Learning to Stand Strong

The political landscape in public health can be ruthless. I've had to push back on pressure, challenge outdated norms, and stay firm in the face of resistance. But it's worth it—when you see a 24/7 pharmacy finally open for the poor, or when a rural hospital gets its first NICU, or when a competent doctor stays on because of better facilities—it's worth every ounce of fight.

Reforming Medical Education: One Module at a Time

As my journey progressed, I found another calling: training the next generation of doctors. I've contributed to the National Medical Commission's new curriculum, especially in subjects like nutrition, demography, and epidemiology—topics that may seem "dry" but are vital for solving real-world health problems.

I'm currently working on a training setup that brings together doctors, public health professionals, and healthcare leaders. It's my way of making sure that the change continues long after I'm gone.

How Doctorpreneur Academy Changed My Perspective

Joining Doctorpreneur Academy gave me a whole new lens. It wasn't just about systems anymore—it was about sustainable models, digital tools, and an entrepreneurial mindset. I learned how to build better teams, streamline operations, and even craft my personal brand to reach more people.

But more than that, I found a community of passionate, mission-driven doctors who dream big, act boldly, and support each other. It has helped me turn my ideas into action faster and more efficiently.

A Mission Bigger Than Me

I've always believed that healthcare doesn't need to be fancy—it needs to be functional. We don't need more gadgets—we need more grit, more heart, more listening.

I'm not here to impress. I'm here to fix what's broken, train those who'll take the baton next, and build systems that serve the many, not just the few.

This is more than my job. It's my movement.

Dr. Neeraj Bedi
MD PSM
Hospital Administrator

CHAPTER 25

HOW I TRANSFORMED MY CLINIC INTO A PATIENT MAGNET!

Dr. Neeraj Saraswat
Dentist and Implantologist
Jaipur

I am Dr. Neeraj Saraswat, a dentist from Jaipur, and my journey has been nothing short of transformative. What began as a conventional dental practice has now evolved into a thriving, patient-centric clinic that stands out in the competitive world of dentistry. My story is one of embracing change, innovation, and entrepreneurial thinking to redefine my approach to dental care.

Discovering My True Potential

Dentistry has always been my passion, but I often felt something was missing. While I was skilled in my craft, I realised that success in dentistry wasn't just about treating patients—it was about creating an ecosystem where patient experience, technology, and strategic growth merged seamlessly.

This realisation hit me when I joined The Doctorpreneur Academy. Here, I was introduced to groundbreaking concepts that expanded my vision beyond the four walls of my clinic. I learned that I wasn't just a dentist; I was an entrepreneur in the healthcare space.

Mastering the Art of Delegation

For years, I believed I had to manage everything on my own—patient care, administration, marketing, and operations. This mindset left me overwhelmed and restricted my clinic's growth. One of the most crucial lessons I learned was the power of delegation.

By building a capable team and trusting them with responsibilities, I was able to focus on what truly mattered—expanding my practice and enhancing patient care. It wasn't easy, but once I learned how to hire, train, and retain the right team members, my clinic flourished like never before.

The Business Side of Dentistry

One of the biggest game-changers for me was understanding the business aspects of running a dental clinic. I delved into:

- Human resource management – Finding the right people and creating a positive work culture.
- Financial planning – Smart budgeting for equipment, marketing, and operations.
- Marketing strategies – Leveraging digital tools to increase my clinic's reach.

Learning from my past mistakes was a crucial step in my growth. I realised that failures weren't setbacks; they were stepping stones that guided me toward better decision-making.

The Digital Transformation

Today's world is digital, and I knew I had to embrace it if I wanted to stay ahead. I began exploring video content creation, website optimisation, and social media marketing. Initially hesitant, I soon discovered the power of online engagement. By educating my audience through videos, blog posts, and patient testimonials, I established credibility and attracted more patients to my clinic.

Search Engine Optimisation (SEO) played a pivotal role in making my clinic more visible online. Instead of relying solely on word-of-mouth, I ensured that patients searching for quality dental care in Jaipur found my clinic at the top of search results.

The Hub and Spoke Model

One of the most innovative strategies I adopted was the hub and spoke model. Instead of limiting my reach to a single location, I expanded by setting up smaller satellite clinics connected to my main centre. This approach allowed me to provide high-quality treatment while making dental care more accessible to a larger population.

Advice for Young Dentists

To those stepping into this field, my advice is simple yet profound:

- Think beyond limits. Success is not confined to traditional practice models.
- Embrace change. The world is evolving, and so should our approach to dentistry.
- Focus on self-improvement. Compete with yourself, refine your skills, and keep learning.

A Journey of Continuous Growth

My journey from a conventional dentist to a visionary entrepreneur has been challenging yet rewarding. Dentistry is no longer just about treating teeth; it's about innovation, leadership, and making a lasting impact in the healthcare industry.

I hope my story inspires others to dream big, take risks, and never stop evolving. If I could transform my clinic into a patient magnet, so can you!

Dr Neeraj Saraswat

Dentist and Implantologist
Jaipur

CHAPTER 26

WHY EVERY DOCTOR MUST DO BRANDING

Dr Neha Singhania
MS, DNB, MRCOG
Gynaecologist, Mumbai

The Journey of My Branding, Independence, and Success in Healthcare

As doctors, we are taught in medical school that our only job is to be an expert in our field. But what we are never taught is how to attract patients in the first place—a million-dollar question.

This is where branding and digital marketing come into the picture. My journey is a testament to how embracing personal branding and digital marketing can transform a doctor's career.

Why Every Doctor Needs to Build a Personal Brand

The age-old belief that "word of mouth is the best publicity" has evolved. Today, it is "word of Google is the best publicity" or simply "you are what Google says you are."

Personal branding is a concept often associated with businesses, but it is equally crucial for medical professionals. A strong personal brand helps build trust and credibility and attracts the right kind of patients. Unlike in corporate hospitals, where a doctor's identity is often overshadowed, personal branding ensures that patients recognise and remember you.

My Roadmap: From Government Hospitals to Corporate Setups to Private Practice

I always wanted to add a personal touch to my practice—what I call "Freedom of Practice." I wanted to offer my patients more without making them wait in long queues at government hospitals, pay exorbitant fees in corporate setups, or be at the mercy of giant insurance companies. But how would patients know my intent? How would the world recognise me?

That's where I leveraged digital marketing. Instead of repeating my message to individuals, I used mass media to announce my presence and build my brand. With guidance from The Doctorpreneur Academy, I learned how to create an online presence, attract patients, and grow my practice.

Do You Need Extra Degrees to Start a Clinic?

No. Of course, staying updated with new treatments and technologies is essential, but that shouldn't stop you from starting your practice.

I believe learning is an ongoing process meant for growth. It should not become an obstacle that delays your success.

How Short Videos Helped Me Attract More Patients

In today's era of "quickest is quirkiest," attention spans are shorter than ever. Even healthcare is not spared from this.

By creating short, simple, and informative videos, I reached a wider audience. Using The Doctorpreneur Academy's strategies, my targeted video ads and strategic content planning generated 5,000 to 6,000 views in a single day.

Thriving as a Freelance Doctor Without Big Hospitals

Working in the corporate sector felt like being a small fish in a vast ocean—without identity, power, or freedom.

For young or first-generation doctors who lack the capital to start their own clinics and do not want to serve big corporate hospitals, freelancing is an excellent alternative. I used branding techniques to establish my name in the market and gain trust, proving that doctors can succeed independently.

How Branding Helped Me Get More Patients

Branding is often mistaken for selling. But it's not about selling; it's about trust and recognition.

Branding is about letting the world know what makes you unique. Any professional who offers their services with a personal touch becomes a brand.

Branding techniques like social media engagement, patient feedback, and educational content helped establish my identity. The Doctorpreneur Academy played a crucial role in guiding me through marketing and patient engagement while helping me avoid common mistakes that new clinic owners make.

Can AI and Online Marketing Be Used Legally for Growth in Private Practice?

The answer is an absolute YES. AI-powered tools can streamline branding efforts.

Today, AI assists in diagnostics, maintains doctor-patient confidentiality, and ensures ethical treatment standards. Doctors can use SEO, paid ads, and social media marketing legally as long as they do not mislead patients or promise guaranteed medical results.

I incorporated AI chatbots, online consultations, and data-driven marketing to enhance patient communication and attract new clients. These digital tools helped me engage with patients without relying on a hospital marketing system.

When done correctly, online marketing improves patient education, builds trust, and expands outreach while staying within legal boundaries.

Making Laparoscopy Affordable for Everyone

Keyhole surgery is available in all major hospitals, but I am working towards making it affordable and accessible for everyone. I advocate for cost-effective laparoscopic procedures to ensure that quality surgical care is available to patients from all economic backgrounds.

Through branding and patient awareness campaigns, I am bridging the gap between expertise and affordability.

My Future Vision

I aim to make advanced surgeries like robotics accessible and affordable for everyone because I firmly believe that socioeconomic status should never determine the quality of healthcare one receives. Healthcare should be choice-driven, even in rural India, not just about what is available at the lowest cost.

Simple Steps for Young Doctors to Start a Clinic

If you are a young doctor considering private practice, follow a structured approach:

1. Gain experience in a hospital setting to build confidence in your clinical skills.
2. Start working on personal branding, digital marketing, and social media skills early in your career with platforms like The Doctorpreneur Academy to establish a strong professional identity.
3. Begin with consultations before investing in a full-fledged clinic.
4. Let people know what you offer through social media and online presence.
5. Communicate in a simple, clear, and jargon-free manner to build trust and improve patient relationships.
6. Seek mentorship from experienced doctors or business professionals to navigate challenges effectively.
7. Use AI and digital tools for patient management and marketing to streamline operations and expand outreach.

8. Offer affordable services while maintaining profitability for long-term sustainability.
9. Stay consistent with branding efforts to grow your reputation over time and establish a thriving independent practice.

Final Thoughts

My journey has proven that branding is essential for doctors who want to succeed beyond the corporate hospital system. The sooner you embrace branding, the better. Waiting for your practice to grow on its own is not a strategy.

The Doctorpreneur Academy provides valuable resources to help doctors like me build their practice, attract more patients, and make a lasting impact in healthcare.

By embracing digital marketing, leveraging AI tools, and focusing on patient engagement, any doctor can follow in my footsteps and carve out their path to success.

Dr Neha Singhania

MS, DNB, MRCOG
Gynaecologist, Mumbai

CHAPTER 27

STRUGGLES TO SUCCESS IN HEALTHCARE-MY STORY OF A HEALER

Dr Nirmala Agarwal
MBBS MD
Infertility and Gynaecology Specialist
New Delhi

*T*he path to success in medicine is filled with trials, but those who stay the course rise as true leaders. My journey has been one of perseverance, adaptability, and forward-thinking in healthcare, and I hope it serves as an inspiration to others.

A Childhood of Challenges and Learning

I began my schooling in Malayalam and only started learning English during my teenage years. When I moved to Delhi for further studies, I faced a significant language barrier. But instead of letting it hold me back, I chose to tackle this challenge head-on. I listened intently, practised consistently, and learned through observation. This experience taught me that dedication and smart strategies can help overcome even the toughest hurdles.

International Exposure: Learning from the Best

With a strong desire to grow, I cleared medical examinations in both the UK and the US. This gave me the opportunity to gain international exposure and collaborate with some of the finest minds in the medical field. These experiences enriched my knowledge and broadened my perspective. Eventually, I returned to India with a mission—to apply what I had learned and serve my own country.

Building a Healthcare Practice in India

Establishing my medical practice in India came with its fair share of difficulties. Setting up a clinic, building credibility, and navigating the healthcare system were challenging tasks. However, my unwavering commitment and hard work led to a thriving career. I have learned that every obstacle can become a stepping stone to greater success.

Personal Growth and Strong Partnerships

Success is not just about professional milestones; it is also about personal growth. My husband and I stood by each other through every trial and triumph, balancing both our personal and professional responsibilities. Our strong partnership became a cornerstone of my success, underscoring the power of support systems in any journey.

A Transformational Experience with The Doctorpreneur Academy

My career took a pivotal turn when I joined The Doctorpreneur Academy. Initially, I was unsure about embracing digital healthcare, but under the mentorship of Dr. Amit Singh and Dr. Pranav Sharma, I found clarity and direction. The structured guidance, expert mentorship, and vibrant community helped me adopt modern business strategies for the medical field.

A significant breakthrough came when I discovered the Plus Program, a dynamic platform that enabled me to seamlessly:

- Conduct coaching programs for doctors
- Share my expertise with a broader audience
- Showcase my talents in poetry and art
- Manage patient care and wellness initiatives

This platform allowed me to blend digital innovation with healthcare, opening new avenues for teaching, healing, and creative expression.

Embracing Digital Healthcare and Coaching

Even with decades of experience, I continue to evolve with the times. Today, I actively engage in telemedicine, digital coaching, and online platforms to connect with more patients and mentor upcoming gynaecologists.

I strongly believe that mentorship is vital in medical practice and always emphasize these guiding principles for young doctors:

- Approach patients with empathy
- Understand their complete health and personal background
- Leverage technology for better care
- Prioritise quality over quantity

Lessons from My Journey

- Stay committed to your goals – With dedication and effort, any barrier can be overcome.
- Embrace continuous learning – Whether it's a new language or technology, growth depends on learning.
- Go digital – The future of healthcare is digital. Adopting it can broaden your impact.
- Value mentorship – Guidance from experienced professionals can shape successful careers.

My journey is a testament to the fact that with the right mindset and mentorship, you can thrive in the ever-evolving world of healthcare. I hope my story inspires others to embrace change, take charge of their careers, and create a meaningful impact.

Dr Nirmala Agarwal

MBBS MD
Infertility and Gynaecology Specialist
New Delhi

CHAPTER 28

HOW I ESTABLISHED A PEDIATRIC SUPER-SPECIALITY HOSPITAL IN LESS THAN 6 MONTHS WITH FEW LOAN LIABILITIES

Dr. Nitin Agrawal
MD Pediatrics, Fellowship in pediatric critical care
Director and Consultant Pediatric Intensivist
The Children's Hospital, Vadodara
Gujarat

A Dream Takes Root

In 1992, I stepped into the world of medicine, driven by a singular passion—to heal children and make a difference. The journey was not without its struggles. Securing the superspeciality I desired proved to be a challenge, but I never allowed setbacks to define my path. Instead, I pushed forward, determined to carve a space for myself in pediatric care.

In 2006, my dream took its first tangible form. I established a small pediatric referral hospital in Vadodara—a 20-bed facility that marked the beginning of a much larger vision. What started as a modest setup soon grew into a trusted name in the community, and with each passing year, my aspirations soared higher.

Building a Strong Team: The Foundation of Success

I quickly realised that no great vision is achieved alone. The key to a thriving medical practise lies in assembling the right team—a team that shares my values, complements my skills, and works towards a common goal.

I was fortunate to form strong partnerships, bringing in colleagues with diverse expertise. Defining clear roles and allowing each partner to contribute meaningfully proved to be a game-changer. The unity and trust among my team members became the driving force behind our collective success.

The Secrets of a Thriving Partnership

Partnerships in business, especially in healthcare, are often riddled with challenges. Through experience, I learned the importance of transparency, fairness, and clear policies. I discovered that an imbalanced revenue distribution can create rifts, and a well-defined, percentage-based model ensures long-term harmony.

My key takeaways for successful partnerships include:

1. Clear communication and alignment of vision.
2. Prioritising experience over image when selecting partners.
3. Matching the velocity of partners to maintain smooth collaboration.

Nurturing and Retaining Staff

Managing human resources in a hospital is no easy feat, but I understood that a happy, well-trained team is the backbone of any medical institution. I emphasised creating a positive work environment, respecting the nursing staff, and ensuring continuous training and professional development.

Beyond salaries, I focused on fostering a culture where employees felt valued and empowered. This, I believe, is the secret to long-term retention and commitment.

The Doctorpreneur Academy: A Guiding Force

The Doctorpreneur Academy played a crucial role in shaping my journey. As an active participant for the past eight months, I have gained invaluable insights, mentorship, and a network of like-minded professionals who have helped me navigate the complexities of expanding a pediatric hospital.

Overcoming Construction and Expansion Challenges

Growing from a rented setup to owning a medical facility was a learning curve filled with unexpected hurdles. From structural limitations to financial liabilities, the transition was not easy. However, I firmly believe that renting initially is a wise decision for a group practice. It allows for flexibility and reduces the burden of fixed expenses.

Through meticulous planning and adaptability, I overcame these challenges, ensuring my hospital continued to expand without compromising on quality.

Marketing: The Often-Overlooked Ingredient for Growth

One of the most important lessons I have learned over two decades in the field is the significance of direct marketing and personal involvement. I built a strong referral base through active engagement with paediatricians and specialists, ensuring that my hospital remained a top choice for patient care.

I also recognised the growing power of digital marketing. While traditional methods of networking still hold value, social media, particularly Facebook and digital outreach, have proven to be crucial tools for reaching a broader audience.

The Power of Fast Decision-Making

In the fast-paced world of healthcare, hesitation can mean lost opportunities. I have realised that swift decision-making—whether in hiring new staff, expanding facilities, or adapting to market shifts—has been one of the key factors in my hospital's success.

A Message to Young Paediatricians

For aspiring paediatricians, I offer a simple but profound message: Plan your career wisely, embrace teamwork, and never stop learning.

I encourage young doctors to focus not just on clinical skills but also on leadership, communication, and strategic thinking. Medicine is not just about treating patients—it's about building systems that provide sustainable, high-quality care.

A Legacy in the Making

Looking ahead, I envision a state-of-the-art pediatric super speciality hospital spanning 10,000 square feet, which has already taken shape. This ambitious project is more than just an expansion; it's a legacy—one that will serve countless children and families in the years to come.

I also plan to transition from intensive care to hospital administration by the time I reach 60, ensuring that the systems I have built continue to thrive even in my absence. I dream of multiple hospitals, with the next generation carrying forward my vision.

Key Insights for Healthcare Entrepreneurs

1. Personal interactions remain the most effective form of direct marketing.
2. Doctors must actively engage in digital media to build visibility.
3. Social media platforms, especially Facebook, offer untapped potential for healthcare branding.

Conclusion

My journey—from a 20-bed pediatric referral hospital to a pediatric super speciality powerhouse—is a testament to perseverance, strategic thinking, and an unwavering commitment to quality care. I hope my story serves as a guiding light for medical professionals looking to step beyond clinical practice and build impactful, patient-centric healthcare institutions.

Dr. Nitin Agrawal.
Pediatric Intensivist
Vadodara, Gujarat

CHAPTER 29

HOW DIGITAL TOOLS HELPED ME GROW MY EYE CLINIC – MY JOURNEY, DR. PANKAJ

Dr. Pankaj Goswami
MBBS, DOMS
Ophthalmologist
Guwahati, Assam.

I still remember the day I stepped out of my job with a modest salary and a heart full of uncertainty. As an ophthalmologist, I knew how to treat eye conditions—but running a clinic? That felt like a different world altogether.

Starting my own eye clinic was a bold move, one driven more by the desire to do something meaningful than by confidence. Initially, I struggled. The patient inflow was minimal. I often sat in my consultation room wondering if I had made a mistake.

But somewhere deep inside, I knew I didn't want to go back. I had to move forward. That's when I stumbled upon Doctorpreneur Academy—and that changed everything.

Embracing Digital Tools – The Turning Point

Joining the academy introduced me to a whole new world. I began learning how to streamline my operations using digital tools—from managing patient records to automating appointment bookings. Everything started becoming more organised, efficient, and surprisingly stress-free. I also learned about systems, SOPs, and how to build a clinic that wasn't just running but growing with clarity.

But the biggest shift wasn't just operational—it was mental. I started seeing myself not just as a doctor but as a healthcare entrepreneur.

From One Clinic to a Nationwide Vision

What began as a small setup has now become something much bigger. I don't just dream of running a clinic anymore—I envision a chain of specialised eye hospitals across India.

And thanks to the practical guidance from Doctorpreneur Academy and the supportive peer group I found there, that dream no longer feels distant. With structured learning and strategic mentorship, I've built the foundation for scalable, compassionate, tech-enabled care.

My Leap into the Digital World

One of the hardest but most rewarding things I did was starting a YouTube channel. Initially, I was extremely shy. Recording videos felt awkward, and public speaking terrified me. But I knew I had to try something different to bring visibility to my clinic.

I started posting educational videos on eye care—simple, genuine content meant to help people understand their vision problems. Slowly, people started noticing. My confidence grew with each video. And over time, that YouTube channel became one of the biggest reasons new patients started walking into my clinic.

Digital content changed everything—it built trust, improved footfall, and gave me a platform to truly connect with my community.

Family: My Unseen Backbone

Behind the scenes, my biggest support has always been my wife. She manages the home and even handles clinic administration. This teamwork has allowed me to stay focused on clinical excellence and long-term growth.

She's the reason I've been able to balance my personal and professional life while still dreaming big.

Training Staff and Enhancing Patient Experience Digitally

As I grew, I realised that I couldn't be everywhere all the time. So I introduced a clinic management app to streamline patient registration and communication. I'm now working on digitally recording staff training modules—so onboarding and upskilling can be consistent across all locations.

These digital systems are helping me deliver quality care at scale, which is vital as I prepare to expand.

A Word to Young Ophthalmologists

If I could speak directly to young doctors entering ophthalmology, I'd say this: Don't wait too long to start your practice. It's not just about earning more—it's about growing personally and professionally. When you build your own brand, create your own systems, and engage directly with patients, you evolve into a better version of yourself. The freedom is unmatched.

Also, I'm a firm believer in the law of attraction. I visualised this life. Positive thoughts and emotional alignment helped me move from fear to clarity.

The Business Side of Eye Care

Of course, the financial part is real. A simple OPD setup needs around ₹15–20 lakhs. A full-fledged OT setup? Around ₹45–50 lakhs. I had to plan every investment carefully.

But my thumb rule is simple: if patient footfall in OPD grows from 5 to 15–20 a day, it's a green signal to expand into surgeries. Growth, I've learned, should be demand-driven and well-planned.

What Doctorpreneur Academy Really Gave Me

More than just business lessons, the Doctorpreneur Academy gave me:

- The courage to speak in front of a camera
- A community of doctors on the same journey
- A blueprint to scale using structured systems
- Insights into branding, communication, and leadership

Above all, it helped me believe in myself again—not just as a clinician, but as a visionary healthcare leader.

Looking Back with Gratitude

Today, when I walk into my clinic, I don't just see patients—I see possibility. I see how far I've come from those anxious early days. My story is not about overnight success. It's about persistence, clarity, and courage.

I am truly grateful for the constant support and encouragement from my parents, my wife, my daughters, and the members of the Doctorpreneur Academy.

I truly believe that with the right digital tools, community, and mindset, any small clinic can become a large-scale mission—not just for patients, but for the doctor who dares to dream.

And if I could do it, so can you.

Dr. Pankaj Goswami

MBBS, DOMS
Ophthalmologist
Guwahati, Assam.

CHAPTER 30

HOW I MADE A DIFFERENCE AS A DENTIST IN REMOTE INDIA – DR. PANKAJ KOHLI'S STORY

Dr.Pankaj Kohli BDS, FETP
Senior Dental Surgeon
Uttarakhand

*I*f someone had told me back in 2005, when I completed my BDS from King George Medical College, that I'd one day be serving in some of the most remote corners of Uttarakhand, I might have smiled and dismissed it. But life had other plans—and I'm glad it did.

The Beginning: More Than Just Dentistry.

Dentistry, for me, was never just about fixing teeth. It was about restoring confidence, relieving pain, and making a tangible difference. After graduating, I joined the government service as a dental surgeon and was later promoted to Senior Dental Surgeon at a district hospital in Dehradun.

But the turning point came in 2007, when I was posted to a hilly, underserved region of Uttarakhand. No glamour, no modern clinics—just a sincere need for care.

Building Something from Almost Nothing.

The place lacked even the basics. No infrastructure, poor access to healthcare, and a general absence of awareness about oral hygiene. But instead of giving in to the limitations, I chose to work with what was available. I coordinated with government authorities, sourced basic equipment, and slowly set up a functioning dental clinic.

I still remember a patient with necrotising fasciitis in 2008 who came to us in critical condition. In that moment, it wasn't just about dental expertise—it was about decisive action, compassion, and staying calm under pressure. We managed to save her life. That moment reminded me why I chose this path.

More Than a Dentist: A Public Health Advocate

Over time, my role expanded beyond the dental chair. I worked as an Assistant Director in the Directorate General of Health & Family Welfare, Dehradun in 2021although it was for a short span, butI took part in projects like Haridwar Mahakumbh Mela control room and deployment of ambulance services for Haridwar Mahakumbh 2021, Moreover, I helped set up oxygen generation plants in Uttarakhand during COVID under the able guidance of senior officials and multidisciplinary teams and spearheaded health awareness campaigns. Inspiring and empowering patients in OPD with knowledge about oral health and advanced dental treatments, fostering a proactive approach to dental care. I didn't want to just serve patients—I wanted to strengthen the system that served them.I am also holding the post of Joint Secretary in the Central Committee of the Provincial Medical Association in Uttarakhand state.

But one challenge remained constant: mindset.

Even after years of service, many still viewed dental care as a luxury. Educating the public became one of my biggest missions.

Embracing Digital for a Wider Impact

That's when I began exploring digital tools—not just for visibility, but to *educate*. I realised that digital platforms could reach people far beyond my physical clinic.

In November 2023, I joined the Doctorpreneur Academy and other online courses. That decision changed everything.

I learned how to:

- Use social media to spread awareness and bust myths.
- Set up systems that made patient care smoother and more efficient.
- Connect with a community of doctors who were not just surviving but thriving.

More than anything, I gained the confidence to dream bigger. I could now see myself not just as a clinician but also as an educator, a communicator, and a leader.

Growth beyond Profession

Outside of work, I prioritise growth in other areas of life too. Whether it's travelling, reading motivational, and positive mindset books. Meeting different people, developing a growth mindset, or even taking dopamine detoxes—I do what it takes to stay sharp and grounded. I've learned to steer clear of negativity and politics, choosing peace and purpose over noise. I also follow the concept of lifelong learning because in this fast-moving world, I believe that if you are standing still, you are moving backwards.

A Message for Young Doctors:

If you're just starting, here's what I want to say:

Start early. Stay grounded. Be patient. And embrace digital tools—they're no longer optional. They're essential.

You don't need a marketing agency to make an impact. You just need the right mindset and some guidance. I found mine through the Doctorpreneur Academy. And if I can do it from the hills of Uttarakhand, you can too.

Dr.Pankaj Kohli BDS, FETP

Dental Surgeon,
Uttarakhand

CHAPTER 31

FROM AVERAGE STUDENT TO COMMUNITY LEADER IN THE FIELD OF AYURVEDA– MY DOCTORPRENEUR JOURNEY

By Vaidya Sanjay Maheshwari
BAMS, PGDYE, DNHE
Hon. Consultant Ayurvedic Physician
Pranav Yoga Ayurveda Healthcare- Mission Mainstreaming Ayurveda.

*I*f you had told me back in school that I'd become an Ayurvedic doctor with international clients and a thriving health and wellness hospital, I might've laughed in disbelief.

I'm Vaidya Sanjay Maheshwari, and I come from the beautiful city of Udaipur. I wasn't born into a family of doctors, and honestly, Ayurveda wasn't even on my radar during my early years.

The Confused Start

॥ आयुःकामयमानेन धर्मार्थसुखसाधनम्। आयुर्वेदोपदेशेषु विधेयः परमादरः ॥

Like many students, I dreamed of becoming an MBBS doctor. I spent three years preparing for PMT exams—and failed. Each year felt heavier than the last. But instead of sinking into despair, I pivoted. I took admission in BAMS. Not out of passion—but because I needed to move forward.

And that's when a new chapter began, though not an easy one.

The first year in my Ayurvedic college was far from inspiring. The environment was dull, the motivation was missing, and I often questioned if I had taken the right path. I felt lost… until something shifted in me.

A Shift in Mindset

In my second year, I decided to stop waiting for inspiration and start creating it. I was observing a common thing that Ayurveda is in demand, but there is a lack of quality care and actual responsible shoulders. I took full responsibility for my future. I began planning my life as a doctor while still in college. I listed out the furniture I'd need for my clinic, what instruments to buy, what my services would be, and even designed my first visiting card.

I didn't wait for a degree to dream—I had already visualised *"Pranav"*. I made a website, mapped out the look of my consultation room, and even decided where each certificate would hang on the wall. My room had become my vision board.

Living the Dream… Step by Step

Money was tight, but my dreams were free. I started small—doing home visits for panchkarma therapies and conducting yoga sessions for a modest fee. It wasn't much, but it was consistent. More than the money, it gave me confidence that this path *could* work.

Then came the big day—my clinic inauguration. It is something like a filmy or biography story, but it's true that I borrowed a panchkarma table, a shirodhara stand, steam chamber from 2 of my friends just to keep at inaugural function, even a chair, a tube light were given by some of the friends. I had no money for the event, not even a day before. That's when a friend stepped in and gave me ₹10,000 without asking anything in return. Me and my juniors and colleges who were volunteering for the inaugural function got boosted with that instant help of 10K, and we restarted preparation from depression to passion. I still get emotional thinking about it.

Over 400 people attended that inauguration. Many became my first patients. And many of them still visit today.

A major turning point in my journey was meeting Deepika—not just as a life partner, but as a true force behind my Doctorpreneurship. I had dreamed of someone who could walk with me in both life and vision, and Deepika exceeded every expectation. With sharp insight and unwavering dedication, she became much more than support—she emerged as the driving force of our hospital. From strategic planning to day-to-day management, she leads with clarity, compassion, and excellence. Today, she not only shares the mission but shapes it, often guiding our growth beyond what I imagined alone.

Thinking Global from Day One

Even as I treated local patients, I always saw myself helping people beyond borders. I once worked part-time at a hotel reception just to observe international tourists—how they thought, how they spoke, what they expected from Ayurveda.

This curiosity turned into connections, and eventually into clientele. Today, I serve patients from Europe, the US and more than 60 countries —not through fancy setups, but through trust, care, and results.

Managing Money and Mindset

I planned everything on a shoestring budget. My clinic expenses were ₹10,000 in the first month. I earned around ₹25,000–₹30,000. That was enough to sustain me and reinvest in growth. No lavish setups, no big banners—just consistent care and careful financial planning.

I had no godfather, no rich legacy—only vision and belief. I created patient brochures, yoga booklets, and Ayurveda guides myself. Every piece of content was a step towards patient empowerment.

The Digital Turning Point – Doctorpreneur Academy

My next big leap came when I joined Doctorpreneur Academy.

Until then, I was managing things manually, intuitively. But the academy showed me how to bring systems, structure, and strategy into my practice.

Here's how it changed the game for me:

- Website & App Launch: I created a personalised app that sends yoga videos, Ayurvedic tips, and post-treatment care—fully automated.

- **100+ Leads in 8 Days:** With the academy's lead generation strategies, I got over 100 quality leads in just over a week.
- **Social Media Made Simple:** Using templates and AI tools, I now manage all digital content in-house without stress.
- **Smooth International Payments:** With integrated gateways, I stopped losing money to failed or delayed payments from global clients.
- **Patient Experience, Upgraded:** My app now sends reminders, tips, and personalised messages—without me lifting a finger.

My Message to You

If you're an Ayurvedic doctor, still wondering *when will my time come?* I have one thing to say: Your time is now.

I started with confusion, came into Ayurveda, was a decision made out of compulsion and ended up building a wellness movement, a mission for mainstreaming Ayurveda, not because I was special, but because I didn't stop. I kept learning, kept building, and kept believing.

If an average student like me can make the journey from an individual practitioner to establishing a full-fledged institution—from running an OPD to managing an IPD, from makeshift "jugaad" solutions to operating a fully NABH-accredited hospital—if I can become one of the first Vaidyas in Udaipur to successfully run a pure private Ayurvedic practice with Panchakarma, and sustain my livelihood solely through Ayurveda (without resorting to mixopathy), then I truly believe anyone can do it.

Doctorpreneur Academy gave me more than just tools—it gave me a tribe, a structure, and the courage to scale with heart.

So don't wait for the perfect time or perfect setup. Start where you are. Use what you have. Do what you can. And do it with vision, heart, and service.

न त्वहं कामये राज्यं न स्वर्गं नापुनर्भवम् । कामये दुःखतप्तानां प्राणिनामार्तिनाशनम् ॥

Vaidya Sanjay Maheshwari

BAMS, PGDYE, DNHE
Hon. Consultant Ayurvedic Physician
Pranav Y Ayurveda Healthcare.
"Mission Mainstreaming Ayurveda"

CHAPTER 32

CANCER SURGEON BALANCING WORK, FAMILY, AND FAITH

Dr. Satish Kamat

MS, DNB, FACRSI

Cancer Surgeon

MUMBAI

*I*f you had met me in the middle of a hectic OPD day or caught me deep in a surgery, you'd probably think I'm just another busy cancer surgeon juggling patients, procedures, and protocols. But there's a rhythm to my life—a pattern that holds everything together. It's shaped by discipline, grounded in family, and guided by faith.

Discipline is My Backbone

I don't believe in glorifying overwork. In fact, I made a conscious decision early on—I won't work beyond 8:30 p.m., no matter how demanding the day has been. My weekends are strictly for family. That's non-negotiable.

I've realised over the years that being a good doctor doesn't mean being *available* all the time—it means being *present*, with your full energy, when it really matters. That's how I protect my sanity, preserve my relationships, and stay sharp in the OT.

Why I Chose Oncology

My journey into medicine was personal. After we lost my father, it was my mother—strong, silent, and steadfast—who shaped my sense of purpose. She never said much, but her presence said everything.

Early in my career, when I saw the kind of suffering cancer brought into families, something shifted in me. I knew I didn't just want to treat patients—I wanted to walk with them through one of the toughest battles of their lives. That's what led me to surgical oncology.

From Scalpel to Robot: Witnessing the Evolution

When I started, open surgeries were the norm. Then came laparoscopy—and now, robotic surgery. The technology has changed dramatically, and I've changed with it.

What hasn't changed is my belief that every surgery, no matter how advanced, needs to be guided by compassion and judgment—not just a user manual. Robotic arms are great, but nothing replaces a surgeon's intuition honed through years of touch and experience.

Private Practice with a Personal Touch

Running a private practice wasn't something I was trained for in med school. But I've always believed that comfort, quality, and integrity must coexist.

My clinic is state-of-the-art, but it's also warm. We respect patient time. We don't chase volume—we build trust. I tell young doctors, "Avoid comparisons. Know your pace. Be punctual. And never forget—you're in a human profession."

Cancer is Never Just Medical

To me, cancer isn't just about tumors. It's about emotions, decisions, fears, finances,and families. Every treatment plan I make is tailored—surgery when it makes sense, not just because it's possible.

Sometimes I even help families explore non-surgical options if I feel that's more humane. It's not always about what I *can* do—it's about what's *right* for the patient at that moment.

The Curse and Gift of Technology

I embrace tech—I use robotics, digital records, and online platforms. But I'm wary of how it's eating into our basic senses.

We used to memorise phone numbers. Now we panic if the battery dies. I see this even in young doctors—too much dependence, too little judgment. The human brain is a beautiful thing. We must train it, trust it, and not outsource it entirely.

Weekends Are Sacred

I work across hospitals during the week, but come the weekend—I switch modes. I play music, meet friends, and spend real, meaningful time with family. No WhatsApp, no scrolling. Just presence.

You see, human connection is medicine too—not just for patients, but for doctors. That's what keeps me grounded.

Friendships Over Fame

I've seen colleagues get lost chasing fame and fortune. But when life hits you hard, it's not your followers—it's your friends who stand by you.

That's why I stay involved with cancer trusts and medical associations. Giving back keeps me humble. Helping underprivileged patients reminds me why I started this journey in the first place.

Families Heal, Too

When someone in the family has cancer, everyone suffers—the kids, the spouse, the caregivers. I've seen families crumble under the weight of silent emotional burdens.

That's why, in my consultations, I make space for everyone. A kind word, a bit of guidance, even listening—it matters. Healing is not just physical. It's emotional, social, and sometimes even spiritual.

No Ego, Only Teamwork

I tell my juniors: drop the ego. We're all on the same side. A good physician, a kind nurse, a diligent admin—all of them matter. There's no hierarchy in healing.

What truly stays with patients is not just your degree—it's how you made them *feel*.

Doctorpreneur Academy: The Game Changer

Joining Doctorpreneur Academy changed a lot for me.

I learned how to manage time without guilt, use digital platforms meaningfully, and structure my practice in a way that reflected *me*. The sessions gave me more than just strategy—they gave me a mindset. I stopped seeing myself as "just a doctor." I started leading like an entrepreneur—with heart.

Now, my practice is more organsed , my team is more aligned, and I get to do what I love without burning out.

At the Core, I'm Human

I may be a surgeon. But before that, I'm a son, a husband, a father, a friend, a believer. My faith helps me stay calm when complications arise. My family reminds me who I am outside the OT.

And my patients? They remind me, every single day, that medicine is not just a science—it's a calling.

I'm Dr. Satish Kamat, and this is my story. I don't just cut cancer out—I walk with people through it. I heal not just with my hands, but with my heart. And if I can do that, so can you.

Dr. Satish Kamat – Cancer Surgeon

MS, DNB ,FACRSI
MUMBAI

CHAPTER 33

START EARLY. HEAL DEEP. THINK DIFFERENT. THE TRUTH ABOUT PSYCHIATRY: WHAT THEY DON'T TELL YOU

Dr. Shubham Sabarwal
MD Psychiatry
Founder, Macflins Mindcare
Psychiatrist | Mental Health Educator | Doctorpreneur

I was 15 when I gave my first mental health session.

I wasn't qualified. I wasn't experienced.

But I cared. And that, it turns out, is the real starting point.

My love affair with the human mind began in school, with a copy of The Power of Your Subconscious Mind book I bought from a railway station. That book didn't just plant seeds—it lit wildfires. At a time when others and I were solving equations and memorising reactions, I was also asking: Why do we suffer silently? Why does no one teach us how to think?

While most teenagers, including myself, were chasing grades, I was also conducting mental health workshops and seminars, helping couples in distress, and helping fellow students lagging to unleash their potential. Back then, I didn't know what I was doing. But I knew why I was doing it.

> To help people see what they were truly capable of.
>
> To stop the silent breakdowns behind smiling faces.
>
> To awaken, not just treat.

That mission hasn't changed.

Medicine of the Mind

As I entered medical school, I explored everything—from the thrill of neurosurgery to the complexity of internal medicine. I cracked some of the toughest entrance exams in India, including NEET, AIIMS, and PGI Chandigarh. In 2020, I stood among the top 20 in the NIMHANS MD Psychiatry entrance, besides topping the Neuromedicine and Neurosurgery papers.

But even with those ranks, psychiatry was never my "backup." It was my choice.

Because nothing mattered more to me than understanding the soul behind the symptoms. When I turned toward psychiatry, I haven't looked back since.

I studied not just psychiatry, but people.

Not just treatments, but transformations.

And while I earned my MD from Medical College, Kolkata, I was also earning something far rarer— clarity of purpose.

The Vision That Wouldn't Let Me Sleep

By the time I finished postgraduation, I knew I didn't just want to practice psychiatry—I wanted to redefine it.

So I founded MACFLINS Mindcare Pvt Ltd—a mental health ecosystem, a clinical company that would combine clinical science with creativity, compassion, and community.

> We weren't going to treat "cases."
>
> We were going to listen to stories.
>
> We weren't going to create lifelong dependents.
>
> We were going to build empowered individuals.

The Bamboo Model of Healing & Digital Outreach: Therapy Meets Technology

Here's how I see it:

> Medication is like bamboo scaffolding—supportive, temporary, necessary at times.
>
> But healing? Healing is about strengthening the structure within.
>
> So that the scaffolding can be removed.

So that the person can stand tall on their own.

This principle drives our anti-dependence, pro-empowerment approach.

That's the foundation of everything we do at MACFLINS Mindcare.

Our packages combine medications, therapy, psychometry, nutrition, music, movement, diagnostics, coaching, and even VR-based interventions.

Through Instagram reels, live Q&As, and AI tools like ChatGPT and Perplexity, I simplify mental health for Gen Z.

We integrate families. We build communities.

And yes—we laugh, sing, and dance too.

A Clinical Venture That Refuses to Create Crutches.

Our model is what I call "self-sabotaging."

We don't encourage lifelong follow-ups. We celebrate graduations.

We don't aim for maximum prescriptions. We aim for maximum freedom.

Some might say that's bad for business.

But I say: It's good for humanity.

And if your business doesn't serve humanity, what's the point?

The Windy Road and the Wisdom It Gave

My doctorpreneurial journey wasn't perfect.

I failed—multiple times—during my MBBS years while trying to start ventures.

I lost money. Lost confidence.

But never lost the fire.

In fact, those failures were my MBA. Every failure taught me the parts of medicine we never get tested on:

Marketing. Communication. Branding. Leadership. Systems. Cashflow Management.

Each fall made my roots stronger. I evolved from just a medico into a doctorpreneur with soul.

Now, I can focus more on patient care while my team handles the numbers, outreach, and backend processes. I also regularly collaborate with pharma companies, educators, and wellness experts to amplify impact. Whether it's a webinar on coping with exam stress or a campaign about mental health in corporations, we believe in collaboration over competition.

The Teachers Who Found Me

Over the years, I've had the immense fortune of learning from giants.

Robert Kiyosaki taught me about wealth.

Blair Singer taught me how to sell with soul.

Sneh Desai and BK Shivani taught me how to coach from the heart.

Dadi Janki, Gaur Gopal Das, and Dr. Deepak Chopra helped me anchor my spirit in science.

With their guidance, I became more than a psychiatrist.

I became a life artist.

A Name I'll Never Forget

During my MD days, in between rounds, therapy sessions, and ward chaos, some of my juniors, maybe jokingly, started calling me "PsychiGod."

It started as light-hearted fun. A nickname. A compliment in disguise.

But it hit me deeper than they probably knew.

Because when people start seeing your work as something sacred,

You start treating it with even more responsibility.

That one word pushed me harder.

To learn more.

Serve better.

Hold space with even greater humility.

So, whether I'm called doctor, dancer, speaker, trainer, founder, or even "PsychiGod"…

My purpose remains the same:

To awaken minds. And set them free.

And what we do isn't just science—it's soul work.

Recognition, Not Just for Me—but for the Movement

I've shared stages with icons- actors, bureaucrats, speakers, and national leaders.

I've been felicitated by the Indian Medical Association for my work.

I've been listed among India's Top 250 Super Speakers.

I've trained thousands of doctors and professionals—online and in person—on how to heal, grow, and build their own healthcare revolutions.

And I've proudly helped NEET/INI-CET aspirants rank AIR 1, 3, 7, 10, and 29—proving that psychiatry, when integrated with leadership and mindset science, changes lives at scale.

But nothing compares to a late-night message that says,

"Doc, I didn't give up on myself because of you."

Or "Doc, you saved our marriage."

That's the moment I live for.

And that's the moment I want every psychiatrist (literally meaning- soul healer) and doctor to experience.

The Future Is Personal

I dream of a future where:

- Mental health clinics feel like wellness sanctuaries
- Patients don't feel judged, but seen
- Young people lead peer-led communities
- Therapists, coaches, and psychiatrists co-create ecosystems of change

And it's happening—through MACFLINS, through VR, through digital outreach, through school and corporate programs, and through every doctor I train to think differently.

A Final Word to the One Reading This:

You don't have to wait for your degree to help someone. Patients want connection, not just credentials.

You don't need to be perfect to begin.

You just need to be willing.

Start early. Heal deep. Think different.

Because psychiatry isn't about illness.

It's about awakening infinite potential.

And the earlier we begin unlocking it, within ourselves and others, the sooner the world starts healing for real.

With love,

Dr. Shubham Sabherwal,

MD, Psychiatry,
Founder-Director, MACFLINS Mindcare Pvt Ltd

CHAPTER 34

DOCTOR. LEADER. DREAMER. THE STORY OF A WOMAN WHO BUILT A LEGACY — IN MY OWN WORDS

Dr. Shubhangi Mundhada
MBBS, M.D (Obstetrics & Gynaecology)
MD, Geetai Hospital, Amravati, Maharashtra

I'm Dr. Shubhangi Mundhada, and if someone had told me back in the 80s that one day I'd not only be running a multispecialty hospital but also mentoring younger doctors and navigating the digital world—I might have laughed in disbelief. But life has a way of shaping us, and I've embraced every phase of the journey with open arms and a determined heart.

The Early Days: Books, Dreams, and B.J. Medical College

My journey into medicine began like many others—with a dream. Growing up in a humble home, daughter of Alaka, and Dr Dinesh Biyani, Dhule, I was always fascinated by the healing power of doctors. When I got into B.J. Medical College, Pune, one of the most prestigious institutions of the time, it felt like the world had opened its arms to me. I secured a 3-year residency in Gynaecology—a rare and coveted opportunity back then.

The training was intense. Long hours, night calls, emotionally heavy emergencies—it was a baptism by fire. But it also shaped me into the clinician I am today. It gave me more than just skills—it gave me resilience, clarity of purpose, and the ability to lead under pressure.

Starting From Scratch in Amravati

In 1988, my husband, Dr O. G. Mundhada, and I returned to Amravati, determined to serve our people and build something of our own. We turned our residential plot into a hospital—not an easy feat in a town with limited infrastructure and resources. I still remember our very first surgery—a simple tubectomy. We had just enough equipment and barely enough staff. But we made it work, and that single case was the seed from which our hospital grew.

My husband, a urologist, was the only one in the region for nearly 25 years. Together, we built a name rooted in trust, consistency, and care.

Brick by Brick: Building a Family, Building a Hospital

Over time, we expanded into a 30-bed hospital, and later, a second 15-bed facility. And now, coming up with a 100-bedded Cancer Hospital for comprehensive cancer treatment and an added multi-speciality unit.

Raised two children while running surgeries and managing emergencies. Each decision I made, I took with one goal in mind: to balance my role as a mother and a doctor.

I consciously adjusted my OPD timings so I could be home when the kids needed me. I even moved to Pune for a time to support my son's academic journey. My children studied in Marathi medium schools—not because it was easy, but because I believed in strong foundational learning. And today, I take pride in watching them thrive: Dr Rohit, a surgical oncologist, and Dr Shantanu Yale-based quantum computing researcher. I am also blessed with a highly educated daughter, in Love, not law, Dr Apoorva and Kanushree. My grandchildren Arya, Arohi ,and Ishan are my Sunshine.

Breaking Ground in Women's Health

While running a full-time practice, I always kept a keen eye on what was needed in Amravati. I introduced endoscopy, brought infertility treatments to the region, and performed the first IUI here. Though I trained in IVF, I couldn't start it myself—but I now mentor my daughter-in-law, Dr Apoorva Gynaecologist and Laparoscopist, who's picking up where I left off.

The Second Innings: Public Health and Purpose

At 59, when most are winding down, I decided to take on a new mission—cervical cancer prevention. I became a certified Colposcopist and now serve as a National Faculty and Master trainer for the FOGSI-IMA HPV vaccination awareness program. My goal is simple but ambitious: help India become cervical cancer-free by 2030.

My work was recognised when I received and am a proud recipient of "Woman of Substance" " Award from Mahesh Professional Forum, Pune.

More Than a Doctor: The Entrepreneur Within

I'll admit—finance and administration weren't my forte initially. But thanks to my husband's early mentorship in money matters, I learned to manage not just patients, but personal finance, hospital renovations, and even agricultural investments. I also pursued a Master's in Hospital Administration, which helped me look at my hospital as more than just a place of healing—it was a legacy.

The Digital Shift: Finding My Tribe at Doctorpreneur Academy

Even with all my clinical experience, I knew the world was changing. I enrolled in a digital marketing course, but it wasn't tailored for someone like me—a doctor with limited time and a different kind of audience. That changed when I joined Doctorpreneur Academy in 2021.

Here, I found more than knowledge—I found community, clarity, and mentorship. I became a Diamond Member, and it helped me not only understand digital tools but use them to grow. Today, I guide younger doctors, implement AI-supported systems in my practice, and feel confident navigating this new world.

Final Reflections

If I could sum up my journey in one line, it would be this:

I didn't just build a hospital—I built a legacy.

And this legacy wasn't just about infrastructure or numbers. It was about impact, compassion, and evolution. From being one of the first Gynaecologists in my region to becoming a mentor and digital learner in my 60s, I've learned that age and background are never barriers when you're purpose-driven.

I hope my story encourages every doctor—especially women—to dream boldly, adapt constantly, and serve wholeheartedly.

Life Moto -Accept Respect and Love, Service to Mankind, She Matters- Care- Educate and Transform, Reduce- Reuse- Recycle to protect the Environment.

Dr. Shubhangi Mundhada

MBBS, M.D (Obstetrics & Gynaecology)
MD Geetai Hospital, Amravati, Maharashtra

CHAPTER 35

HOW SOCIAL MEDIA TRANSFORMED MY DERMATOLOGY PRACTICE – MY STORY AS DR. SIVARANJANI

Dr. Sivaranjani
Dermatologist
Villupuram, Chennai.

I'm Dr. Sivaranjani, a dermatologist practising in Villupuram, a quiet yet bustling town just a few hours away from Chennai. My journey into the world of skincare, healing, and digital empowerment wasn't something I had planned—but looking back, it's been nothing short of magical.

From a Bookworm to a Skin Specialist

I've always been a studious girl—my father, a strong influence in my life, nudged me toward medicine, and I happily followed. I completed my MBBS in 2014, and it was during those years that I found myself drawn to skin issues. Every time I saw a patient with dermatological concerns, I felt this inner curiosity spark. That spark became a passion, and soon, dermatology became my chosen path—with a special love for cosmetology.

Starting Out with Hope and Setbacks

Like many of us, my early days in practice weren't glamorous. I shared a small clinic with a colleague, trying to find my footing. And then—COVID hit.

It was disorienting. Momentum vanished. But somewhere inside, I knew this was the moment to reinvent, not retreat.

After the pandemic, I took a leap of faith and opened my own clinic—this time, thoughtfully. I chose a space right opposite the government hospital, knowing the visibility and accessibility would help. I ensured patients had a comfortable waiting area, especially since some procedures took time.

My husband, a surgeon, stood by me like a rock—helping out with surgical dermatology cases like cyst removals, PRF for ulcers, and minor suturing. His support meant the world to me.

From Acne to Aesthetics – Offering Complete Skin Care

Today, my clinic isn't just about skin—it's about confidence. We offer:

- Laser hair removal
- Acne and scar treatments

- Pigmentation correction
- PRP and PRF therapy for hair and skin rejuvenation
- Chronic ulcer treatments

This blend of clinical dermatology and aesthetic care became our signature style—and patients started noticing.

The Day Everything Changed – My Digital Awakening

One day, I got a WhatsApp message about Doctorpreneur Academy. Honestly, I didn't think much of it—but I clicked. That click changed my entire perspective.

With no background in marketing or tech, I was hesitant. But the way the academy broke things down was so practical and doable. I jumped into the 30-Day Reels Challenge, started editing videos, making posts, and learning how to truly connect with patients—digitally.

Even when I took a break from posting for a year, new patients kept showing up—thanks to my older content. The compound effect was real. People thought I had hired a marketing team—but the truth is, I did it all myself.

And I loved every second of it.

From 3 Patients to 30+ a Day

When I first started, I had days with just 3 or 4 patients. Now, I see 30–35 patients daily—and many come in because they saw a reel or a post, or read a review online.

They tell me, "I saw how you do the procedure—I feel I can trust you."

That trust is everything.

The Dream Ahead – A Cosmetology Centre

Now, I'm planning the next chapter: a dedicated cosmetology wing. A place that's more than a clinic—it'll be a wellness space where patients walk in not just for treatment, but for transformation.

The Family behind the Scenes

My husband didn't realise how deep I was diving into the digital space until he saw the results. Now, he's proud. My daughters are my cheerleaders. They'd often ask, "Amma, how are you learning all this alone?"

I smile and say, "Because I'm not alone. I have a Doctorpreneur Academy."

What Doctorpreneur Academy Taught Me

- That social media isn't just for trends—it's a trust-building tool
- That I can build a brand without spending lakhs on marketing
- That patients are already online—I just needed to show up
- That confidence doesn't come from ads, but from authenticity

Final Words

To every doctor wondering if digital is your thing—let me tell you: if I could do it with zero background, so can you.

You don't need a marketing team. You need the right mindset, the right mentor, and a little courage.

Today, I am not just a dermatologist. I'm a digitally empowered healer. And if you're reading this, maybe it's your time to start too.

Dr. Sivaranjani
Dermatologist
Villupuram, Chennai.

CHAPTER 36

FROM GOVERNMENT DUTY TO PRIVATE PRACTICE: MY JOURNEY OF SERVICE, GROWTH & LEGACY

Dr. S. R. Sharma
MBBS MS GENERAL SURGERY
Solan, Himachal Pradesh

I was born in a small village tucked away in the hills of Hamirpur, Himachal Pradesh. Ours was a simple life — surrounded by nature, steeped in tradition, and grounded in values. I wasn't someone who grew up dreaming of being a doctor. In fact, becoming a doctor seemed like a faraway idea, almost unreachable. But life has a way of nudging you toward your path, and for me, that nudge came from my elder brother — a pharmacist whose dedication and discipline quietly shaped my ambitions.

With his encouragement and my family's unwavering support, I pursued my studies seriously. I cleared the pre-medical entrance and found myself in Punjab, selected for MBBS at a reputed college. That journey from a rural classroom to a medical college campus was transformative. I went on to complete my MS in General Surgery there as well. During my house job, I even dabbled briefly in dermatology, but it was surgery that truly spoke to me — the precision, the responsibility, the immediate impact you could have on someone's life.

Two Decades in Government Service: My First Calling

In the early 1980s, I joined the Himachal Pradesh government health services. Back then, government postings often meant you had to serve in the remotest of areas — and I did. I was posted across the length and breadth of Himachal: from the interiors of Mandi to the tough terrains of Mandi and Sirmaur. We had limited resources, no specialists nearby, and yet the expectations of the people were immense.

I performed a wide range of general surgeries and, when required, orthopaedic procedures too. I vividly remember conducting complex surgeries without the advanced tools we take for granted today. But what we lacked in resources, we made up for with commitment. We were healers, but also problem-solvers, decision-makers, and sometimes — just compassionate listeners.

For 20 years, I served the people of Himachal with honesty and heart. But as time passed and my children grew up and stepped into their own medical careers, I began reflecting on the next chapter of my life. I wanted stability — freedom from transfers and the occasional political interference that came with government service.

A New Chapter: Private Practice in Solan

With my wife, a dedicated gynaecologist by my side, I took voluntary retirement and decided to start a private practice in Solan. We weren't building just a clinic — we were creating a space that combined professionalism with compassion, expertise with affordability. Slowly and steadily, we earned the trust of the community.

Our patients came not just from Solan, but from neighbouring towns and villages. We didn't believe in flashy marketing — our work spoke for us. The biggest compliment? When a patient would say, "I trust you like family."

A Family of Healers

As years went by, something beautiful happened — our medical legacy began to take root. My son, now a skilled general surgeon, joined the practice. My daughter became a pathologist at a reputed diagnostic centre, and my daughter-in-law, a talented dermatologist, completed the circle.

Today, what we've built isn't just a hospital. It's a home of healing, run by a family that lives and breathes medicine.

Affordable, Ethical, and Evolving

One principle I've always believed in is this: medicine is a service, not a business. Our hospital's pricing has always been mindful of the common man's pocket. We've never compromised on quality — but we've always ensured accessibility.

Over the years, we've upgraded our facilities, introduced new specialties, and focused on improving patient care. But growth never came at the cost of ethics. Every decision we made was rooted in transparency and patient welfare.

Learning Never Stops: My Journey with Doctorpreneur Academy

Even with decades of experience, I've never stopped learning. That's what brought me to the Doctorpreneur Academy. The healthcare landscape is evolving rapidly, and I realised that to sustain and scale ethically, we needed systems, structure, and the power of digital tools.

Through the academy, I gained insights into:

- Setting up systems for smoother practice management
- Leveraging digital tools for better outreach
- Creating workflows to reduce dependency
- Understanding branding and communication in the digital era

What struck me the most was how relevant all this was — even for someone with a full-fledged hospital. We began working on digital visibility, rethinking our patient engagement strategies, and streamlining our operations. It was like giving a new engine to a car that had already run well — now we could go farther, faster, and more efficiently.

Final Thoughts: Legacy, Not Just Practice

Today, I stand proud — not just because of the surgeries I've performed or the hospital we've built, but because of the lives we've touched and the values we've upheld. If I could share one message with young doctors, it would be this:

"Be patient. Give yourself time to grow after specialisation. Learn with humility, serve with integrity, and always, always keep learning."

I am grateful for this journey — from a village in Himachal to a legacy of healthcare that's still growing. And I'm thankful to the Doctorpreneur Academy for helping me see what's possible when traditional wisdom meets modern tools.

Dr. S. R. Sharma
MBBS MS GENERAL SURGERY
Solan, Himachal Pradesh

CHAPTER 37

REDEFINING WOMEN'S HEALTHCARE THROUGH INNOVATION, RESILIENCE & LEADERSHIP

Dr. Sumana Talakokkula
MBBS, DA, DGO
Obstetrics and Gynaecologist
Bengaluru

Wearing multiple hats

From the operating theatre to the boardroom, my journey has been anything but conventional. Along the way, I've worn many hats—clinician, hospital administrator, stroke survivor, tech enthusiast, mother, and mentor. But at the heart of it all, I've always remained deeply connected to one purpose: transforming women's healthcare through innovation, empathy, and leadership.

A Vision Born in Practice

Some careers unfold gradually. Mine unfolded through fire—through seismic shifts and unexpected turns. I was barely in my 20s when I was handed the reins of a 70-beded hospital. I was still finding my footing as an obstetrician-gynaecologist, and suddenly I was managing operations, people, and systems. It was intense, yes—but it also laid the foundation for my journey into systems thinking, leadership, and a broader view of healthcare delivery.

Broadening My Horizons: From India to the World

As I progressed clinically, I felt a strong urge to expand my perspective. I pursued fellowships in Germany and the United States—not just to refine my surgical skills in laparoscopy but to learn how healthcare could be more humane, more efficient, more patient-centric. What I witnessed abroad was the seamless integration of care, compassion, and technology. That exposure fueled my hunger for lifelong learning and deepened my curiosity about the future of gynaecology.

When the Healer Became the Patient

Just as my career was picking up pace, life threw me a curveball. After the birth of my second child, I suffered a stroke. The diagnosis was right-sided paralysis and facial palsy. I went from doctor to patient in a heartbeat. It was terrifying. But it was also transformative. I discovered a strength I didn't know I had. Through relentless physiotherapy, emotional grit, and the unconditional love of my children, I made a full recovery.

That chapter changed me. It made me more grounded, more empathetic. I began to listen to my patients more closely—not just their symptoms, but their silences.

The Digital Shift: From Clinician to AI Evangelist

As healthcare started embracing digital innovation, I knew I had to evolve too. I dove into the world of Artificial Intelligence in medicine—not as a trend follower, but as a learner and implementer. I took up certifications, explored tools that could enhance diagnostics, and implemented AI-driven systems to improve patient engagement and safety.

My efforts were recognised internationally. I was even interviewed at a healthcare summit in Dubai. But more than the recognition, it was the realisation that AI can amplify our compassion—not replace it—that kept me going.

Pioneering Aesthetic & Regenerative Gynaecology

I've always believed that healthcare should evolve with the needs of the people we serve. That belief led me to explore the emerging space of aesthetic and regenerative gynaecology. From PRP therapy to non-surgical vaginal rejuvenation, I embraced new techniques to help women feel confident, comfortable, and empowered.

It's not just about appearance—it's about agency. When women reclaim ownership of their bodies, the ripple effect touches every aspect of their lives.

Bridging Medicine and Management

Even as I practised, I knew that true transformation needed strategic insight. That's why I enrolled in a healthcare management program at IIM Trichy. It's helping me bridge two worlds—the science of care and the business of sustainable, scalable healthcare.

Today, I serve as the Head of OBGYN at SLG Hospital and Senior Consultant at Apollo Kondapur. I mentor young doctors, lead digital transformation projects, and push for a more compassionate model of care—every single day.

Celebrating Milestones, But Staying Grounded

Over the years, I've been humbled by awards and recognitions:

- Outstanding Leadership Award – Health 2.0 Conference
- Excellence in Clinical Practice – Bharath Leadership Excellence
- Most Loved Place to Work – Apollo Health & Lifestyle

I've conducted workshops, spoken at international forums, and led programs in fertility care and minimally invasive surgery. But more than accolades, it's the patient smiles, the regained confidence, the lives touched—that keep me rooted.

Leading with Heart

Degrees and designations aside, I believe leadership is an inside-out process. I start every day with mindfulness and gratitude. I encourage the same for my colleagues—because in the rush to serve others, we often forget to care for ourselves.

True leadership isn't about control—it's about lifting others, especially during their most vulnerable moments.

My Message to the Next Generation of Doctors

- Be fearless in learning—because medicine is evolving faster than ever.
- Specialise with purpose—your niche will become your voice.
- Innovate with compassion—technology should serve humanity, not overshadow it.
- Lead with empathy—because it's your strongest currency in the long run.

A Life Still Unfolding

My journey is far from over. I envision a healthcare ecosystem where women are treated not just for their symptoms—but uplifted, educated, and empowered at every touchpoint. Where innovation meets empathy. Where healing is holistic.

I didn't set out to be a changemaker. But maybe that's how it begins—one decision, one patient, one purpose at a time.

Dr. Sumana Talakokkula

Obstetrics and Gynaecologist
Bengaluru

CHAPTER 38

THE POWER OF DEDICATION & FAMILY SUPPORT IN MY JOURNEY AS A SURGEON, MENTOR, AND HUMAN

Dr. Suneet Sud
MBBS MS Gen. Surgery
FMAS, DNB, MRCS-I, FIAGES, FACRSI, MNIMS, FEHS
Safal Hospital Nagpur

I've often believed that every doctor carries not just a degree, but a story. Mine began not in the grandeur of operating theatres, but in the quiet trials of personal setbacks and the unwavering strength of family.

From Struggle to Stability: The Early Days

My early journey in medicine wasn't smooth. After setting up my practice, I made a few financial decisions that, in hindsight, lacked planning. Loan repayments kept piling up, and I wasn't financially equipped to handle them until 2024. It was a stressful time, but it taught me some of the most important lessons of my life—discipline, patience, and the need to marry purpose with planning.

But those hard days didn't break me—they built me. Every challenge pushed me to think more critically, manage more consciously, and serve more sincerely.

Family: My Silent Strength

I grew up in a family where medicine wasn't just a profession—it was a way of life. My father, an orthopaedic surgeon, was not just my inspiration but also my guidepost. Watching him serve patients with compassion laid the foundation for my own calling as a surgeon.

When I started, my father and sister—she's a gynaecologist—stood beside me like pillars. My clinic was set up adjacent to theirs, creating an ecosystem of collaboration and support. There were days when patients would come asking for my father instead of me, and I don't blame them—he was the trusted name in town. But I quietly kept showing up, giving each patient the kind of honest, dedicated care they deserved.

Slowly, people began to see me. Not just as Dr. Sud's son, but as *Dr. Suneet Sud*—a surgeon who would listen, explain, and operate with integrity.

Choosing Integrity, Every Single Time

In our field, there's constant pressure to give in to external influences—cutting ethical corners for quicker success. But I made a decision early on: I would never compromise on values. I've said "no" to many requests that didn't sit right with my conscience. I believe that long-term trust is always more valuable than short-term gain.

Ironically, it was my financial struggle that pushed me to learn more—not just about surgery, but about how to *run* a practice. I began exploring finance, business models, and sustainability. That knowledge gave me the confidence to grow without selling my soul.

Giving Back: My Why

Today, I do much more than operate. I teach surgery at a homoeopathic medical college—not for money, but because I want to shape future doctors. I've also trained health workers in rural areas in basic surgical care. Sometimes, improving one stitch in a village clinic can save a life.

There's one story that's particularly close to my heart—a bright young student I came across who couldn't afford medical education. I decided to sponsor his studies. I've been there, I know what it means to be held back by finances. Helping him is my way of giving what I wish I had.

And we're just getting started. I'm now working on expanding our hospital's impact globally through teleconsultations—bridging the gap between local expertise and international access.

Doctorpreneur Academy: The Turning Point

One of the most transformational chapters in my journey was joining *The Doctorpreneur Academy*. Until then, I was surviving—but they taught me how to grow *strategically*. Through the academy, I learned:

- How to run a practice like a business—with heart and systems
- How to market ethically, and build a credible digital presence
- How to form a strong doctor network that supports and mentors
- And most importantly, how to see healthcare not just as a service, but a *movement*

That's when my mindset shifted from "being a good surgeon" to becoming a *healthcare leader with a purpose.*

Creating a Safe Space for Learning

I believe in mentorship without ego. I regularly host academic webinars and invite young doctors to reach out. If my experiences can save someone else a year of struggle—or a mistake—I feel it's my duty to share.

Final Thoughts: A Surgeon, With Soul

At the end of the day, my identity isn't just in how many surgeries I perform—it's in the lives I've touched, the students I've mentored, and the patients who trust me. I'm here not just to operate, but to uplift. To pass on what I've learned. To show that success in medicine is not just about skill—it's about soul, systems, and service.

And for that, I will always remain a grateful student of life, family, and purpose.

Dr. Suneet Sud

MBBS MS Gen. Surgery

CHAPTER 39

PIONEERING HEALTHCARE: MY JOURNEY FROM CLINICIAN TO INNOVATOR ENTREPRENEUR

Dr. T J Pradeep Kumar
Consultant Physician, Cardio-Diabetologist, and Critical Care Expert
Medical Director & CEO at Brookefield Hospital, Bengaluru

Brookefield Hospital: A Journey of Vision, Dedication, and Innovation

Bengaluru, known for its thriving tech scene, is also home to cutting-edge healthcare facilities, thanks to passionate professionals like my wife, Dr.

Sangeeta, and me, Dr. T J Pradeep Kumar. As a Consultant Physician, Cardio-Diabetologist, and Critical Care Expert, I have always believed in pushing boundaries in healthcare. My wife, a BDS and M.Sc. in Clinical Research, shares the same passion for medical excellence.

Together, we built Brookefield Hospital, a 100-bed multispecialty healthcare facility. Our journey—from humble beginnings to leading a state-of-the-art hospital—has been filled with challenges, learning, and relentless determination.

Roots in Vatrak: Initial Training and Service

My journey began far from Bengaluru, in Vatrak, a rural area 80 kilometres from Ahmedabad. After completing my postgraduate studies at JMM Medical College, Davangere, in 1999, I joined a peripheral health centre there. The experience was intense—I treated everything from snake bites to heart attacks with minimal resources. It was here that I built my confidence, resilience, and ability to think on my feet.

Initially, my wife, Dr. Sangeeta, was hesitant to join me in this rural setting. But after our marriage, she embraced the practice wholeheartedly. We formed deep connections with the local community, and soon, they saw us as lifesavers. These years strengthened our commitment to making quality healthcare accessible to all.

Back to Bengaluru: Returning to the City of Dreams

After two enriching years, we returned to Bengaluru with a vision for greater impact. I joined Vydehi Institute of Medical Sciences, focusing on teaching and administration. However, I soon realised that I was feeling stagnant. My wife and I decided to step into group practise and corporate health checkups, launching 'First Consultants' and 'First Health'.

While these ventures were ahead of their time, they taught us valuable lessons about timing and entrepreneurship. We knew we wanted to build something bigger—a hospital that would redefine patient care.

Brookefield Hospital: The Birth of a Dream

Starting a 100-bed hospital with limited financial resources was a daunting task. But with unwavering family support and strategic planning, we turned our dream into reality.

In 2010, Brookefield Hospital was launched with 60 beds. Over the years, it has evolved into a leading multispecialty healthcare facility, attracting patients from across the city. It was not just about building a hospital—it was about creating a healthcare ecosystem driven by quality, compassion, and innovation.

Building a Strong Team

Our hospital's success rests on the shoulders of a dedicated and passionate team. While my wife, Dr. Sangeeta, oversees day-to-day operations, I focus on patient care and strategic growth. We strongly believe in fostering a collaborative environment, which has been key to our hospital's continued excellence.

Step-by-Step Implementation: Overcoming Challenges

Creating Brookefield Hospital required meticulous planning and execution. Every decision was made with long-term sustainability in mind. We ensured that financial stability, operational efficiency, and patient-centric care remained our top priorities. Our ability to turn challenges into opportunities has been a cornerstone of our journey.

Innovative Critical Care – Project BEAST

One of my proudest achievements is Project BEAST (Brookefield Emergency and Accident Support Team). This initiative was designed to revolutionise emergency response. Instead of relying solely on ambulances, we introduced:

- ICU-equipped two-wheelers with trained paramedics
- App-based emergency response technology
- Faster intervention during the crucial 'golden hour'

With over 2,500 patients treated, Project BEAST has proven its impact. We are now working on expanding it nationally, ensuring that more lives are saved with this rapid-response model.

Investing in Life: Pioneering a New Approach to Saving Lives

Project BEAST reflects my commitment to making critical care more accessible. By bringing ICU-level treatment to patients' doorsteps, we have addressed a major challenge—delayed medical intervention due to urban traffic congestion.

This initiative has not only improved survival rates but also set a new benchmark in pre-hospital emergency care.

Words for Future Healers: My Advice to Young Doctors

Throughout my journey, I have learned valuable lessons that I hope to pass on to aspiring doctors and healthcare entrepreneurs:

- Perseverance is key – Challenges will come, but persistence will see you through.
- Continuous learning is essential – Medicine is constantly evolving; stay updated.
- Adaptability is everything – The world of healthcare is unpredictable—be ready to embrace change.

- Seek out opportunities – Growth comes when you step out of your comfort zone.

A Bright Future Ahead

Looking ahead, we plan to expand Brookefield Hospital to 200 beds and introduce new specialties like cardiology and infertility services. Our mission is to continue pushing the boundaries of medical excellence, making quality healthcare accessible, innovative, and patient-focused.

Final Thoughts: The Power of Vision and Dedication

Our journey from rural healthcare providers to urban hospital pioneers is a testament to the power of vision, dedication, and resilience. My wife and I believe that extraordinary things are possible when you have the right support, a clear mission, and an unwavering commitment to making a difference.

As we continue to set new benchmarks in healthcare, we hope to inspire the next generation of doctors to take bold steps, embrace innovation, and create a meaningful impact in the world of medicine.

Dr. T J Pradeep Kumar

Consultant Physician, Cardio-Diabetologist, and Critical Care Expert
Medical Director & CEO at Brookefield Hospital, Bengaluru

CHAPTER 40

FROM HOMEMAKER TO HEALTHCARE CEO: MY JOURNEY BEHIND VARDHAN FERTILITY'S GROWTH

Vaibhavi, CEO
Vardhan Fertility & Laparoscopy
Women's Care Centre,
Bengaluru

When people walk into our clinic, they usually expect the man in the white coat to be running the show. But behind the scenes of Vardhan

Fertility & Laparoscopy Women's Care Centre in Bengaluru, I wear a different kind of coat—that of a *visionary, problem solver, and CEO*. I'm Vaibhavi, and while I may not be a doctor, I have dedicated my life to building one of the most trusted fertility centres in the region.

The Journey of Vardhan: A Story of Love, Support, and Excellence

As a former MSC Maths teacher with a background in Material Science, I never imagined that I would one day become the CEO and Counsellor of a renowned fertility centre. But life had other plans. When I married Dr. Vijaykumar P K, a gifted surgeon, I knew that I had found my partner in every sense of the word. Initially, I found it challenging to understand the technical and surgical jargon, but I was determined to support my husband and become his backbone.

I left my government job to dedicate myself to my husband's work, and it was one of the best decisions I ever made. While I miss teaching mathematics to students, I have found a new passion in my role at Vardhan. As CEO and Counsellor, I have the privilege of working closely with IVF patients, providing them with confidence and hope during a challenging time in their lives.

A Journey Rooted in Purpose

My journey into healthcare didn't begin in a boardroom—it began at home, supporting my husband, Dr. Vijaykumar PK, in his mission to make quality fertility care accessible and compassionate. Over time, as his clinical practice grew, so did the need for strong systems, structure, patient care pathways, team management, and trust-building.

That's when I stepped in—not just as a spouse, but as a *strategic partner* and eventually the CEO of Vardhan Fertility.

The Man Behind the Science: Dr. Vijaykumar PK

While I lead operations, it's my husband who leads the science. Dr. Vijaykumar PK is the Director of Vardhan Fertility and Laparoscopy Women's Care Centre in Bengaluru, Karnataka. With 18 years of experience in Obstetrics and Gynaecology—and over 12 years deeply rooted in Infertility, ART, and Laparoscopy—he is the heart of our clinical expertise.

He has independently conducted numerous IVF/ICSI cycles from stimulation to transfer, and is known for his hardworking nature, sincerity, and team spirit. He's on a mission to evolve as a Gynaec Laparoscopic Surgeon, with a deep interest in Andrology, Reproductive Medicine, and evidence-based clinical research.

His calm demeanour and people-first attitude have made him a trusted name—not just among his patients, but also his peers. Together, we form the perfect team—he brings the science, and I bring the structure.

Dr. Vijaykumar P K's schedule is incredibly demanding, with 5-10 operative laparoscopy cases every day. He travels extensively to perform surgeries in Kerala, Tamil Nadu, Andhra Pradesh, and various locations in Karnataka. The sheer volume of surgeries he performs is staggering – imagine the number of procedures he has completed in a month, a year, and over the course of 25 years!

My Role: Building Systems That Empower Healing

When I took over as CEO, I knew my job wasn't just about running a clinic—it was about *building an ecosystem* of hope and healing. We worked hard to:

- Streamline patient journeys
- Create compassionate counselling protocols

- Build a high-performing, emotionally intelligent team
- Get NABH accreditation
- Ensure transparency and emotional support at every touchpoint

Empathy Before Appointments

Infertility is a deeply personal journey. I've met couples shattered by failed cycles and broken trust. At Vardhan, our mission is not just to offer treatments—but to restore belief.

Every patient is welcomed with warmth, not paperwork. We walk them through the journey, simplify the science, and most importantly—we never treat them like a number.

We've designed *customised counselling systems*, especially for patients who come after failed IVF or IUI cycles. We help them process what went wrong, and only then do we speak about what's next. That kind of support changes outcomes. I've seen it firsthand.

For the past 12 years, I have personally counselled countless IVF patients, and it gives me immense pleasure to see them overcome their struggles and achieve their dreams of parenthood. My husband, Dr. Vijaykumar P K, is a highly acclaimed surgeon with over 30 years of experience. He is renowned as one of the best surgeons in South India, and his expertise in operative laparoscopy is unmatched.

Training with Heart

We hire slow and train deep. Each new team member goes through a 15-day observation period—not just to assess skill, but to understand if they *truly care.*

We take feedback seriously. Monthly training sessions, patient reviews, and constant communication help us build a *culture* of excellence. We aren't just treating patients—we're building *relationships.*

Leading with Clarity (and Calm)

Today, we operate two branches, manage a 45-member team, and see a steady flow of patients who come to us through word of mouth, referrals, and most recently—YouTube.

That's right—our Vardhan Fertility YouTube channel has become a digital doorway for patients to learn about fertility, bust myths, and understand options—*even before they walk into our clinic*. I personally script many of the videos, ensuring the tone is reassuring, simple, and empowering.

From Family Support to a Scalable Brand

Vardhan is more than just a fertility centre to me – it's like my baby. I am committed to ensuring that it continues to thrive and provide hope to those who need it most. As I look back on our journey, I am filled with a sense of pride and purpose. I am grateful to be a part of this incredible team and to play a role in helping couples achieve their dreams of parenthood.

What began as supporting my husband's dream has now grown into a full-fledged brand. But I didn't do it alone.

I credit a big part of this structured growth to the Doctorpreneur Academy. Through the academy, I learned:

- How to run operations like a business without losing empathy
- How to build a team culture that retains talent
- How to use digital presence to build trust
- How to make data-driven decisions without micromanaging doctors

Their ecosystem gave me the clarity and tools I needed to scale responsibly, and sustainably.

My Message to Other Healthcare Wives and Women Entrepreneurs

You don't need an MBBS to make a difference in healthcare. Whether you're a doctor's wife, a healthcare administrator, or just someone with a dream—your *role is powerful.*

My message is simple: Trust your vision. Learn the ropes. Build systems. Bring empathy. And show up every single day.

Because behind every successful clinic isn't just a great doctor—it's also a great *leader* holding it all together.

Vaibhavi, CEO

Vardhan Fertility & Laparoscopy
Women's Care Centre,
Bengaluru

To serve is human.

To heal is divine.

To do both—that is the heart of the Doctorpreneur.

ABOUT THE DOCTORPRENEUR ACADEMY

THE DOCTORPRENEUR ACADEMY
Empowering Doctors to Serve Humanity Better

*T*he Doctorpreneur Academy is an honest and genuine effort to help doctors cope with the changing healthcare landscape. It is their safe place where they can learn, implement, fail, re-learn, ask for help & guidance, and network without being judged. Above all, this is a place where they will be encouraged to follow their dreams rather than ridiculed for being different, as happens in the outside world. They get all the necessary knowledge, systems, tools, processes, community and mentorship in one place!

Our mission is simple yet powerful:

To empower doctors across all systems of medicine — Allopathy, Homoeopathy, Ayurveda, Dentistry, Physiotherapy, etc. — with the skills, tools, systems, and mentorship they were never taught in medical school.

For too long, doctors in India have been overlooked by a healthcare system that assumes they "know it all" and don't need support.

But the truth is — doctors are the core of India's healthcare ecosystem, and they need guidance beyond clinical skills to thrive in today's fast-evolving landscape.

That's why we built The Doctorpreneur Academy — a platform designed to empower doctors with the knowledge, tools, and systems they were never taught, but truly need.

We believe the real key to transforming India's healthcare system doesn't lie solely with government or corporate hospitals — but with **doctor-led, mid-sized hospitals** (up to 150 beds), run by local physicians who understand and care for their communities deeply.

This model creates a **win-win for all stakeholders**:

- **Patients** receive personalized care — the kind that's often missing in large corporate setups.
- **Doctors** are free from quarterly profit pressures and can focus on healing, leading to a more fulfilling and balanced professional life.
- **Governments** benefit too, as these doctor-led units can bridge the gap in underserved regions where quality healthcare infrastructure is still a distant dream.
- Even in metros, where corporate hospitals dominate, they often remain inaccessible to a large section of the population — here too, doctor-led hospitals can make a massive difference.

But building and running such hospitals isn't easy. Clinical expertise alone isn't enough. It demands leadership, systems, business acumen, and resilience.

That's where The Doctorpreneur Academy steps in — to empower doctors with the tools, skills, systems, and community support they need to start, build, and scale successful clinics and hospitals.

Because when doctors lead the way, India heals better.

The Academy serves as a catalyst for this transformation by offering:

1. **Digital Academy:** Comprehensive courses tailored for healthcare professionals.
2. **Online Community:** A collaborative space for doctors to connect and share knowledge.
3. **Consulting Services:** Expert guidance for clinic and hospital growth.
4. **Innovative Software:** Solutions designed to address real-world healthcare challenges.

It is a unique approach to help doctors validate by a strong **community of 20,000+ members of the community.**

We believe:

- A happy and empowered doctor = better patient outcomes
- And better outcomes = a healthier India 🇮🇳

If that resonates with you — whether you're a doctor, dreamer, founder, or investor — we'd love to connect.

Let's make healthcare in India stronger, together.

Grateful for your time.

Thanks

Dr Pranav Sharma
Amit Singh Moga
The Doctorpreneur Academy
(https://www.thedoctorpreneuracademy.com)

FOUNDERS OF THE DOCTORPRENEUR ACADEMY

Dr Pranav Sharma
MBBS, MS, MCh (CTVS, AIIMS, DELHI)
Director, The Doctorpreneur Academy,
Former Chief Medical Administrator (CMA) & Professor of Cardiac Surgery at U.N. Mehta Institute of Cardiology & Research Centre, Ahmedabad.

Dr Pranav Sharma has completed his medical education from AIIMS Delhi, where he specialised in cardio-vascular surgeries. After completing his education at AIIMS, he started a career at U.N. Mehta Institute of Cardiology & Research Centre, Ahmedabad. Rising the corporate ladder, he became the Chief Medical Administrator at U.N. Mehta, where he oversaw the expansion of the hospital from 100 beds to 1200 beds in a very short span of time. After his stint in the corporate world, he decided to do something different and independent and start his own healthcare consultancy, where he has helped hundreds of doctors and other healthcare professionals to open up new hospitals/clinics/nursing homes across India. He is based out of Ahmedabad.

Early Life

Born into a humble, middle-class family with a strong legacy in medicine — a father who was an Ayurvedic physician and a grandfather who practised as a General Physician — the path to a career in healthcare felt almost destined for him.

He pursued his medical education at **AIIMS Delhi**, specialising in cardiovascular surgery. Upon completion, he began his career at the prestigious **U.N. Mehta Institute of Cardiology & Research Centre** in Ahmedabad.

But life took an unexpected turn.

In the early years of his career, he was diagnosed with **Young Onset Parkinson's Disease (YOPD)** — a devastating diagnosis for a surgeon whose hands were his greatest asset. The news shattered him. Yet, rather than give in, he chose to fight back.

Over the next decade, he transitioned from being a surgeon to a professor and eventually to a highly respected medical administrator. While his professional journey was accelerating, so was the progression of the disease. He began experiencing severe side effects from the 20+ pills he was taking daily — the medication had become more punishing than the disease itself.

After years of physical and emotional turmoil, he made a courageous decision: to undergo **Deep Brain Stimulation (DBS)** — a high-risk, 16-hour surgery that eventually brought the disease under control.

The rebirth with the grace of God

Not just a physical transformation, but a spiritual awakening. He saw this second chance as a divine signal — a call to dedicate his life to a greater cause. With a renewed sense of purpose, he set out to transform India's healthcare ecosystem — not through hospitals or policy, but by **empowering doctors themselves**.

And that's how the **seed of The Doctorpreneur Academy** was planted — a bold initiative to support doctors and healthcare professionals with the tools, systems, and mindset needed to lead, grow, and build the healthcare institutions India truly needs.

You can contact him at drpranav@thedoctorpreneuracademy.com

LinkedIn-https://www.linkedin.com/in/drpranavsharma21/

Amit Singh Moga,

Ph.D (Healthcare, France), MBA (IIM Ahmedabad), B.Tech (IIT Roorkee)
Director, The Doctorpreneur Academy
Former Scientist, Ex-Banker, Author, TEDx Speaker, Serial Entrepreneur

Ex-Scientist, A former Banker, an Author (The Black Book) and TEDx Speaker, Mr. Amit Singh has done multiple things in a short span of time. Wearing multiple hats, Mr Amit Singh is an entrepreneur at heart. Being an engineer and MBA from India's top institutes, it was very easy to rise in the corporate world and live in his comfort zone, but he decided to travel the road less taken. After spending 10 years in the corporate world, last being a banker where he oversees many big healthcare projects being funded, he quit the job world and started his entrepreneurship journey in the world of healthcare. He is also based out of Ahmedabad.

Life isn't always a bed of roses — not even for IIT and IIM graduates. It's a common misconception. Everyone carries a story, and his is one of grit, grief, and growth.

Born into a middle-class North Indian family, his path was clear from the start — like many others, he had three career options: Engineer, Doctor, or IAS Officer. He chose engineering, graduated from **IIT Roorkee**, and began his career as a **Scientist at DRDO**.

At the time, he was preparing for the civil services, but life had other plans. In 2008, a **freak accident** changed everything — he lost his beloved mother within a span of 14 days. The sudden loss turned his world upside down. What followed was a long, silent battle with **depression**, a darkness he didn't fully recognise until it had consumed him.

It took **five years** to rise from that pain, to heal, and to find clarity.

In 2013, after years of struggle and introspection, he cracked the entrance to **IIM Ahmedabad** and joined the prestigious **2-year PGP program** — a rare feat, as he entered campus with both his **wife and 3-year-old child**. His unconventional journey broke stereotypes and made headlines in **The Times of India, Business Standard, Career360, and Economic Times**, inspiring many to rethink what's possible.

In 2015, he joined **YES BANK as AVP**, based in Mumbai. Yet within a year, it became clear: the corporate world wasn't his calling. Despite the financial security, he felt a growing **vacuum** — a deep sense of **restlessness** and lack of purpose.

Then came the turning point.

In 2016, he had his **eureka moment**. What he was truly seeking wasn't just success — it was **FREEDOM**. Freedom to choose his path, own his time, design his life, and build something meaningful. He left his high-paying job and stepped into the world of entrepreneurship — **with no business background, no roadmap, and no safety net**.

Just one thing: a burning desire to make a difference.

Today, he is the co-founder of **The Doctorpreneur Academy** — the world's **first digital community** for doctors focused on **entrepreneurship and leadership**. An ecosystem built to empower doctors across India with the tools, systems, and mindset they were never taught in medical school.

He is also building **DocAngels** — a bold initiative to create the **world's largest network of doctors and healthcare professionals investing in startups** as angel investors.

From surviving loss and battling depression, to redefining success and building impact-driven ventures, his journey is a testament to the power of purpose, resilience, and reinvention.

You can contact him at dramit@thedoctorpreneuracademy.com

LinkedIn- https://www.linkedin.com/in/dramitsinghmoga/

Disclosure

This book, "I Can Heal: Stories of Real Doctors. Real Sacrifices. Real Impact" (Volume 1), is a heartfelt compilation of real-life journeys, published by The Doctorpreneur Academy. These stories—shared by the author and other contributors—shine a light on the courage, vulnerability, and purpose that define the lives of doctors across India.

Each story has been voluntarily submitted and personally approved by the respective authors, who have chosen to share their experiences to inspire and uplift others. The contributors are solely responsible for the content of their submissions.

Please note: The experiences, outcomes, and transformations described in this book are personal and exceptional. They are not intended as promises or guarantees. We do not and cannot make assurances about your ability to replicate these results using the ideas, tools, strategies, courses, or training materials discussed herein. Your results depend entirely on your own actions, commitment, and circumstances.

This book offers proven insights, strategies, and reflections that have worked for the authors, *The Doctorpreneur Academy*, and its members. While we believe these can guide and support you in your journey, success ultimately comes from within—driven by your choices and efforts.

To learn more about our community, our policies, and to review our disclaimers, terms of service, and privacy guidelines, please visit:

🌐 www.thedoctorpreneuracademy.com

We value transparency, authenticity, and integrity in everything we do.

Thank you for choosing to engage with this book—we hope it brings you powerful insights, fresh inspiration, and the spark to pursue your own path of growth and healing.

If that resonates with you — whether you're a doctor, dreamer, founder, or investor — we'd love to connect.

Let's make healthcare in India stronger, together.

Dr Pranav Sharma
MBBS, MS, MCh (CTVS, AIIMS, DELHI)
Director, The Doctorpreneur Academy
Former Chief Medical Administrator (CMA) & Professor of Cardiac Surgery at U.N. Mehta Institute of Cardiology & Research Centre, Ahmedabad.

Amit Singh Moga
Ph.D (Healthcare, France), MBA (IIM Ahmedabad), B.Tech (IIT Roorkee)
Director, The Doctorpreneur Academy
Former Scientist, Ex-Banker, Author, TEDx Speaker, Serial Entrepreneur

The Doctorpreneur Academy

Scan and Connect

www.thedoctopreneuracademy.com

THE DOCTOPRENEUR ACADEMY

www.ingramcontent.com/pod-product-compliance
Lightning Source LLC
LaVergne TN
LVHW061543070526
838199LV00077B/6879